GOTHIC LONG ISLAND

HAUNTED LEGENDS AND GHOSTLY SIGHTINGS

ANGELA ARTUSO

AMERICA
THROUGH
TIME

America Through Time
Fonthill Media Inc.
www.through-time.com

First published 2025
Copyright © Angela Artuso 2025

ISBN 978-1-62545-156-9

All rights reserved. No part of this publication may be reproduced, stored in a retrieval system or transmitted in any form or by any means, electronic, mechanical, photocopying, recording or otherwise, without prior permission in writing from Fonthill Media Inc.

Typeset in 10pt on 13pt Sabon
Printed and bound in England

All images were taken by the author unless otherwise noted.

Contents

Introduction   5

1	Bethpage Village Restoration, Old Bethpage, New York	9
2	Camp Hero, Montauk, New York	13
3	Execution Rocks Lighthouse, Long Island Sound, New York	17
4	Fiorello Dolce, Huntington, New York	20
5	Fire Island Lighthouse, Fire Island, New York	23
6	Goody Garlick and the Long Island Witch Trials, East Hampton, New York	26
7	Harbor Mist Restaurant, Cold Spring Harbor, New York	29
8	Katie's Bar of Smithtown, Smithtown, New York	34
9	The Terry-Ketcham Inn, Center Moriches, New York	39
10	Lake Ronkonkoma, Ronkonkoma, New York	41
11	Lakeview Cemetery, Patchogue, New York	43
12	Montauk Lighthouse, Montauk, New York	54
13	Montauk Manor, Montauk, New York	60
14	Mount Misery and Sweet Hollow Road, Melville, New York	64
15	Oheka Castle, Cold Spring Harbor, New York	69
16	Old Burying Ground in Huntington, Old Burying Ground and Fort Golgotha, Huntington, New York	73
17	Popper the Poltergeist, Seaford, New York	80
18	Raynham Hall, Oyster Bay, New York	86
19	Roxey the LIRR Dog, Mineola, New York	98
20	Sagtikos Manor, Bay Shore, New York	105
21	The Country House Restaurant, Stony Brook, New York	107
22	The Gateway Playhouse, Bellport, New York	109
23	The Wickham Farmhouse, Cutchogue, New York	111
24	Vail-Leavitt Music Hall, Riverhead, New York	113
25	Winfield Hall, Glen Cove, New York	116

Bibliography   122

INTRODUCTION

There is nothing like the thrill of a chilling, well-spun ghost story, and this book will introduce you to some of the most popular and interesting haunted locations on Long Island. But what is it about ghost stories, spooky places, and ghostly legends that keep us coming back for more thrills and chills? We all have that innate curiosity that drives us to explore the unknown, and ghost stories offer that open window into the ultimate mystery of what lies beyond our time here on Earth. No matter how old you are or what you believe about the paranormal and hauntings, there will always be countless ghost stories passed down through generations. Many of these tales originate from specific places that are said to be haunted over the years and many have experienced tumultuous times in history. These stories and experiences offer a glimpse into the unknown that has fascinated people for ages.

Psychologists have found that spooky stories tap into our primal fears and anxieties, allowing us to face them in a controlled environment. Engaging with these tales can be a cathartic experience, providing a safe space to confront our dread and ponder existential questions without real-world consequences. How many of us have had unexplainable occurrences, seen ghostly apparitions, had a visit from a deceased loved one? If you are one of those people, you will definitely remember how terrified you were. When we're young, occurrences like this don't come with a handbook of instructions. Many of us grow up thinking there is something wrong with us until we get older and find out there are many others out there who have had the same experiences. Many of us are left questioning if these mean something bad is going to happen to us or end up leaving a person with nonstop fear, hoping they will never have these experiences again. We have had numerous people reach out to us for help and guidance with situations like these ranging from parents who have young children claiming to be visited by people walking into their rooms in the middle of the night to astro physicists who see dead relatives in their home. The paranormal has no boundaries. There will always be legends that will be passed down for generations as well as your classic ghost story that can defy basic human understanding. This confrontation with the incomprehensible is both terrifying and exhilarating but at the same time can be very calming once you begin to understand what is that you're experiencing and why it could be happening. People in general tend to be frightened of things they do not understand.

Your classic ghost stories are often interwoven with significant historical events that took place. Local ghost lore can reflect a society's collective guilt, traumas, or even the unresolved conflicts of the dead from historical injustices. Gettysburg, one of the most haunted locations in the United States, is a classic example of that. These tales preserve the past while breathing life into the morals and consequences of events that have shaped a community. In many cultures, ghost stories teach morality and to be mindful of things that could come back to haunt you (no pun intended).

In today's world, the media, TV, and film industry have played a huge role in how the paranormal is perceived and amplifies the reach and impact of ghost stories as well as shock value. However, many shows and video channels sensationalize their content to get a larger viewing audience, which can cause confusion and fear among people who are genuinely seeking help. A true, experienced paranormal investigator knows that many of these things shown on social media just do not happen the way these people portray them. Many of those people just want to create terror and fear for popularity rather than helping people understand what they're truly experiencing. This also causes an issue for people who desperately want to reach out for help but are absolutely terrified to do so because of what they think will happen based on falsely portrayed content. I can't tell you how many times people have told us how surprised they were by what actually takes place during a paranormal investigation and what it's really like. There are many honest and truthful paranormal investigators out there who truly want nothing more than to help educate people and help them make sense of what they're experiencing. Investigations into your home and business are free—and should be free. If someone is charging you several hundred dollars to come look at the equipment they use and guarantee that they will rid your ghost for $2,000, run and find yourself another investigator. Charlatans are out there ready to take advantage so be cautious. Special events at haunted locations are fun to attend, especially for newcomers because they provide you with a nice basic introduction to what takes place during an investigation. More like a class and tour of a haunted site, fees are usually minimal and help cover the cost for insurance, location fee, and materials.

Researching and visiting haunted locations can be quite a time-consuming endeavor. Records on a location can often be challenging to find due to various reasons such as fires, property demolitions, or inadequate record-keeping. Before embarking on any visits, research is essential. This includes delving into the land history, property background, and the stories of the individuals linked to the location. Despite encountering dead ends during the research process, a simple search in the right place can sometimes unveil long-forgotten family names and events. The amount of work involved in research is often underestimated until one delves into it. There are several crucial things to keep in mind while compiling your research. Names may have different spellings across various time periods, and property names might change with new owners. Through this process, you might stumble upon answers to long-standing questions. Historical archives, firsthand testimonies, and even conducting interviews with locals are all part of the research journey. Online platforms like libraries, history websites, online blogs, author sites, ancestry records, census records, etc., can all offer valuable insights and generate leads to new information by providing dates, names, locations and so much more.

It is important to remember that while the research process can be captivating, showing respect towards these locations and their histories comes first. Two fundamental rules in the realm of the paranormal are to always show respect and never trespass. Understanding the legends and stories associated with haunted locations is a key aspect of the research. Distinguishing between fact and fiction is crucial, as many popular ghost tales may have been embellished or fabricated over time and this is always something that one has to remember. Another thing to keep in mind is that some people and locations just don't want it plastered publicly that they have paranormal activity at their location even though they do. This could be because their location may host children or those with special needs. Others don't want it publicized because they don't want to deal with thrill seekers who have no regard for personal property bombarding their establishment. For some, it could be related to religious beliefs, or they might not want to be teased or made fun of by others in the community. The reasons vary and are different for each one. Whatever the reason, it is important to be respectful of that.

Let's dive into what exactly constitutes a haunted location. Is it just an old, abandoned house, or can any place be considered haunted? The truth is, there is no definitive answer. Haunted locations can range from historic buildings and offices to modern homes. It could be a wooded area or even a lake. It could be a train or plane. Some even claim to have objects that are haunted. It could be anything. Many times, it's just the person that is "haunted" and not the location. One of the biggest questions in the paranormal world is why some locations are haunted, and others are not. In researching paranormal activity over the years, activity can sometimes be linked to emotion. Locations with extreme emotional events and tumultuous histories seem to carry over that residual emotional energy over the years more than those without. Some locations are associated with tragic events such as murders, suicides, or natural disasters. Others may have a connection to famous figures or historical events. Whatever the case may be, these stories and events add to the mystery and intrigue of these places. These are not just abandoned buildings or tourist attractions; they are places that hold immense significance to the spirits who reside there. So always remember to show respect and treat these locations with care.

As you continuously explore haunted locations, you may begin to feel more connected to the energies and spirits that inhabit them. This can be a fascinating and enlightening experience, but it is important to always prioritize your safety and well-being. When visiting haunted locations, safety should be your top priority. Pay attention to any unusual occurrences or sensations during your visit, such as inexplicable noises, sudden cold drafts, or the feeling of being watched. Make note of these experiences and document them for future reference. One very important rule to remember is to never investigate alone. The reason is that if you fall and get hurt in a rundown location that has broken concrete, broken steps, etc., no one will know you are there, making it difficult for you to get help. Another reason is that if you do encounter some strange, unexplainable activity, it would be great to have another person witness that with you to get their take on what is actually happening and if it truly is paranormal.

Haunted locations often attract a lot of attention, which can have both positive and negative effects on local communities. On the one hand, it can bring in tourism and boost the economy. On the other hand, it can also disrupt the everyday lives of those living in these communities. It is important to be mindful and respectful of the local community when visiting haunted locations. This includes being considerate of noise levels, following any designated parking or visiting hours, never trespassing, and supporting local businesses during your stay. Paranormal research and investigating potentially haunted locations requires an open mind and a willingness to believe in things beyond our understanding. With careful planning, respect, and an open mind, you may just uncover the mysteries that lie within these hauntingly beautiful places. Many of the public locations and workspaces are also someone's livelihood so one should always be respectful and mindful of that.

As a researcher, it is important to approach haunted locations with respect, sensitivity, and responsibility. This means refraining from any disrespectful or harmful activities such as vandalism or provoking spirits. Provoking during an investigation can have huge ramifications for the families and those living and working on the property. If you provoke to get a rise out of the spirits and force them to communicate, you leave the family to face the consequences once the investigation is over and you leave so don't do it. Conducting a responsible investigation also involves proper research and documentation of the location's history and reported hauntings. This helps provide a deeper understanding of the location and its potential paranormal activity.

I've spent over two decades researching and visiting haunted locations. It has become a passion and labor of love. Helping others try to understand their experiences has been very fulfilling over the years. I've been an active member of the TAPS Family as well as TAPS Family Co-Manager. TAPS, short for The Atlantic Paranormal Society, is the team of investigators featured on the popular TV shows *Ghost Hunters* and *Ghost Nation*. As more locations opened up about their ghostly inhabitants and their need for help, investigations flourished, and my involvement, personally as well as with my team, deepened.

If you find yourself near any of these locations, feel free to explore them. Many are very kind and welcoming establishments eager to share their stories, while others carry folklore and ghostly legends for you to ponder. Haunted histories for many locations are often posted on their websites for enthusiasts to enjoy, as well as opening times, tour information, and any special events they might have. Visiting these locations and supporting them helps keep them around for future generations to enjoy.

Remember, ghosts were people, too.

Happy Hauntings!

Bethpage Village Restoration, Old Bethpage, New York

In 1963, Nassau County embarked on an ambitious endeavor to acquire the Powell farm, a sprawling 165-acre property brimming with historical significance. The story of Old Bethpage Village Restoration is a tale of preservation dedicated to the restoration and preservation of the region's architectural heritage of Long Island's rich history with the intent to create a development of historic restoration of many of the area's landmarks. The process of bringing Old Bethpage Village Restoration to life was no small feat. Historical buildings and homes, each with its own unique story to tell, were carefully selected and transported to the site. Some structures were lifted intact, while others were dismantled and reassembled piece by piece once they arrived at the village. The village officially opened to the public in 1970.

Old Bethpage Village Restoration is comprised of nineteen historical buildings and homes that were once located elsewhere on Long Island and all from many diverse backgrounds. Each one of these historic structures has brought with them their own set of unique legends. Some of the structures include a farmhouse, a hat shop, a general store, an inn, and a blacksmith shop. These are just a few of the many structures one can visit in the village. Some of the homes have been reported to have unexplainable occurrences that defy explanation. Others claim to hear voices and other unexplainable noises. Many claim that many of these structures are haunted. Is it just urban legend or is it really haunted?

The Conklin House

The Conklin House is an old fisherman's cottage. It came to the village from the Village of the Branches, which is a town located in Smithtown, Long Island. Visitors have reported hearing unexplainable banging sounds echoing through its halls, while sightings of a woman dressed in period clothing are said to be seen on the stairs on the upper floor, leaving many unsettled. Dark moving shapes have been seen and loud bangs have also been reported. Joseph H. Conklin was married to Thankful Hallock and bought the home in 1853. Thankful Hallock was the niece of Thomas Hallock who used to own an inn that was once next door to the Conklin house at its original site before it came to the village. It is rumored that Walt Whitman was one of the home's earliest tenants.

The Conklin House.

The Noon Inn

According to the *Long Island Herald* on July 23, 1920, John H. Noon and his wife, Mary Ann Pelt, purchased the inn on September 2, 1848. It was originally located on the corner of East Meadow Avenue (formerly Newbridge Avenue) and Prospect Avenue (formerly Hay Carters Lane) in East Meadow where it stood for about 132 years. Shortly after he purchased it, he changed the name to Wells Fargo Hotel. Noon was a resident of Hempstead and purchased other inns, one in Farmingdale and another in Plainedge. He ended up selling the East Meadow Inn in 1859.

On June 8, 1883, German-born Heinrich Schultz and his wife, Lena, purchased the inn, which then became known as the Schultz Hotel. Lena died shortly after the purchase, and Heinrich took a new wife named Adelina Hoffman in 1890.

On January 5, 1914, the inn was then sold to Andrew Hoeffner who was a farmer in a town called Foster's Meadow, otherwise known today as Elmont. The inn was known at that time as the East Meadow Hotel, also known as the A. Hoeffner Hotel. Andrew and his wife had nine children, and they were strongly considering closing the inn, which he eventually did, especially with the prohibition in the 1920s. Once the inn closed, the Hoeffner family returned to farming, and everyone in the home worked on the farm. By 1955, the home was no longer being used as a residence, and in 1962, Clifford Hoeffner offered the house for free on behalf of the family, along with the sum of $500 to be used to move the residence and keep it as a museum.

The Noon Inn was originally built as an inn and a bar. It eventually closed and ended up being used for storage. According to local lore, a tragic incident involving a homeless man and three teenagers has left an indelible mark on the inn's history.

Urban legend states that a homeless person was sleeping inside the building when it was used for storage. Three teenagers broke in while the homeless man was sleeping.

The Noon Inn.

Startled by the teens, the homeless man ended up killing all three of them, one upstairs and two downstairs. The bodies were eventually discovered, and the homeless man confessed to the killings. It was reported that a girl was visiting the house and saw the images of the three males in one of the upstairs windows. This was supposedly reported the same night that the homeless man hanged himself in jail. Reports of slamming doors and windows, along with objects mysteriously moving, hint at a restless spirit still lingering within its walls.

The Williams House

There have been reports of doors and windows slamming throughout the house, and objects moving. It is said that a worker heard a ghostly voice telling her to "put my teacup down" while she was cleaning the area.

The Hewlett House

The Hewlett House was originally built in the 1890s in Woodbury. Strange noises and voices had been heard in the basement by security guards, but no one was there. A worker reported feeling a hand placed on her shoulder, and once again, no one was there. A worker claims to have seen the initials of Lewis Hewlett carved into the ceiling above the fireplace after being tapped on the shoulder. This was the first time the initials were discovered as they never had been reportedly seen by anybody there before that incident. Others have reported a strong feeling of being drawn to the stairs.

The Louis Ritch Farmhouse

The Louis Ritch Farmhouse was originally from Middle Island. It was owned by Louis Ritch, his wife, Charity, and their six children. The house is said to be visited by Louis Ritch who died in 1835 and walks around the porch in heavy boots.

The only building that was there originally is the Powell Farmhouse. The first building that was moved to the village was the Manetto Hill Methodist Church which came from Plainview and dates back to 1857.

A visit to the Old Bethpage Village Restoration takes you back in time to a nineteenth-century village, allowing you to explore at your own pace its historic buildings, each with their own history that whispers visions from the past. Whether you are a history buff, a lover of folklore, or simply in search of a lingering spirit or apparition or two, Old Bethpage Village Restoration is a great outdoor place to visit. Their website lists their hours of operation along with any special upcoming events that they may have planned.

2

CAMP HERO, MONTAUK, NEW YORK

One of the biggest enigmas on Long Island is Camp Hero in Montauk. It is believed to have inspired the well-known series *Stranger Things* and has been surrounded by secrecy and intrigue for many years. The tales linked to it are not your typical spooky ghost stories. In some respects, the rumored stories of Camp Hero are even more chilling.

Camp Hero was believed to have served as a previous U.S. Air Force base, yet numerous individuals are convinced that it conceals scientific studies and mysterious non-human beings kept hidden from the public eye. Among the most prominent conspiracy theories linked to Camp Hero is the notion that the site has been utilized for top-secret government and military experiments, investigations into extraterrestrial life, and even research on time manipulation. This conspiracy theory is famously referred to as the Montauk Project.

Camp Hero has served as a site for a multitude of training exercises throughout history, playing a role in the Revolutionary War, the War of 1812, the Spanish-American War, World War I, and World War II. Following its involvement in World War II, the camp transitioned into a coastal defense station dedicated to safeguarding the New York coast.

There have been numerous rumors over the years that Camp Hero was housing aliens in underground bunkers and conducting mind-control exercises on humans. In a *New York Post* article dated October 24, 2020, written by Dana Kennedy, she interviewed a gentleman named Joe Loffreno, who claimed to have been abducted and abused in 1980 when he was a young boy around the age of twelve or thirteen. He described in the interview that while under hypnosis he was able to remember being invited by a local boy to ride bikes over to the base. Loffreno was quoted as saying, "I was hypnotized by a certified hypnotist for about 40 minutes and all these memories flooded back. They did a very bad thing to us out there. We were just little kids. They had no right to experiment on us. It was a very dark, very evil thing." He goes on to say in the article, "They analyzed us like animals." He states that there were up to fifty other children in there and believes some of them may have been killed later on. Loffreno believes that he is one of the "Montauk Boys" that were mentioned in the book *The Montauk Project: Experiments in Time* written by Preston Nichols.

View of Camp Hero from the lighthouse.

In addition to the Montauk Project, there is also another story called the Philadelphia Experiment. It is said that in the fall of 1943, the USS *Eldrige*, a U.S. Navy destroyer, was made invisible and teleported via time travel from Philadelphia to Virginia. The experiment was said to have taken a horrible twist where during the reappearance of the ship, many of the sailors were embedded into sections of the ship and suffered an agonizing death. This incident was known as the Philadelphia Experiment. It has been said that the crew of the civilian merchant ship SS *Andrew Furuseth* witnessed the USS *Eldrige*'s arrival as it was being teleported in Virginia. All documents of the event were reviewed in detail and later changed to them denying seeing any such incident. Records in the Archives Branch of the Naval History and Heritage Command have been repeatedly searched, but no documents have ever been found.

An odd story was reported in 2009, when *Dan's Papers* reported that the police had received a call from a local resident named Howard Edelstein, who lived in the Camp Hero housing development, which was a mile away from the radar tower at Camp Hero. He told the police that when he woke up, he observed the dish on top of the tower had moved about 90 degrees counterclockwise from where it was the night before. The man stated that the radar dish had not moved since 1966. The Montauk Police Annex sent an officer to investigate but the officer could not remember if the dish was pointed any differently from where it always had been pointed. They began asking others if they knew which direction the dish had been pointed and several people were very adamant about it pointing northeast. The police had called the New York State Parks Commission who checked the plans and found the radar tower was, indeed, pointing northeast in 2002. Believing now that it had indeed been moved, they then called the Montauk Fire Department for the possibility that it might have become loose from its original moorings on top of the concrete tower. The fire department tried to set up ladders alongside the tower, but the ladders would not reach. Deeming it unsafe for them to continue in case the radar tower was loose and getting ready to topple, they abandoned their mission and sought further help from the New York City Bridge and Flange Repair Company, which would send a crew that was to arrive in about two days. During this time, the radar dish once again moved another 90 degrees during the night.

The team of experts at the New York City Bridge and Flange Repair Company were able to climb the tower and reported that there was no movement whatsoever and the radar dish was completely intact. They examined all the heavy bolts and found that even though the bolts were a bit rusted, they were still holding it quite strongly in position and there was no danger at all of it falling or coming loose.

Still trying to find an answer, a call was then made to experts in the military who would look at the blueprints of the interior of the tower to see if they could go inside and see what could have possibly caused it to move. A crew of police officers, Coast Guard Air Rescue, Army Engineers, and several other experts established a plan to go inside and see what could have come loose. They stated that the interior was completely frozen solid, and it was impossible for anything in there to move causing the dish to turn. Everyone was completely baffled as there was no explanation as to why the radar dish would move, and why it would move at exactly 90 degrees. Police officers stayed

Camp Hero radar tower.

that night to see if they could catch sight of the dish moving, but it did not move that night.

The town supervisor ordered the watch to be discontinued due to budget concerns. The cause of the movement of the radar dish was never found and there have been no reports of it moving ever since.

Camp Hero State Park is a National Historic Site open to the public although the military site of Camp Hero is sealed off with numerous ominous warning signs throughout the area. The stories of mind control experiments, aliens, secret labs, time travel, and secret undergrown tunnels are just a few of the many rumors that have been shared over the years and have always been denied by the military. It is said that Camp Hero is haunted by non-human spirits and strange, unsettling creatures that have been tortured and tormented and still roam the area and have never found peace. If you are planning to visit Camp Hero State Park, I recommend checking their website first for more detailed information about the park and a detailed map which is available for you to download. The park covers 450 acres of land, including beachfront and heavily wooded areas. Please note that the military section is restricted to visitors.

3

Execution Rocks Lighthouse, Long Island Sound, New York

Execution Rocks is a manmade island made of granite on a rock-filled reef, created in 1949. It is situated in Long Island Sound, between New Rochelle and Sands Point, New York. It stands at 62 feet tall, and is 1,400 feet from the shore.

Adjacent to the island is a two-story building that was used to house caretakers until 1979 when it became automated. The living conditions for the lighthouse keepers were extremely poor before automation. Initially, they resided at the base of the lighthouse tower, enduring cold, dampness, and frequent flooding caused by leaks and cracks. In 1866, a separate building was constructed for the keepers' quarters. With the lighthouse's automation in 1979, there was no longer a need for keepers to remain on the island.

There are a few legends that surround the lighthouse and how it got its name, Execution Rocks. One legend has it that there were several shipwrecks and deaths that occurred caused by its rocks and shallow waters. Another legend has it that British soldiers chained their prisoners to the rocks during the Revolutionary War. They were chained during low tide and left there to drown as the tide rose. It is also rumored that early colonists would chain those who committed crimes punishable by death to the rocks and leave the bodies there long after they were dead for onlookers to witness.

One popular legend is that of a serial killer named Carl Panzram who died in 1930. He was a vicious and gruesome killer who raped and murdered over twenty men and boys and boasted how he would kill anyone who bothered or simply annoyed him. He confessed to twenty-one murders and thousands of robberies. His gruesome resume also includes over 1,000 acts of sodomy and numerous accounts of arson. He escaped from just about every single prison he was sentenced to.

His ongoing captures and escapes did not seem to slow him down, and the murder spree continued throughout the States all the way to Africa and back again. He escaped from numerous prisons only to be captured over and over again. His last prison stay was at Leavenworth Federal Penitentiary where he was sentenced to death after beating a laundry worker to death with an iron bar. He was hanged for his murderous crimes on September 5, 1930. A year before his death, he wrote an autobiography while on death row entitled *Killer: A Journal of Murder* which was released detailing his murderous rampages and how proud he was of each and every one of his killings. In addition to his

Execution Rocks lighthouse, 1931. (*Photo credit: National Archives and Records Administration, Public domain, via Wikimedia Commons*)

Execution Rocks Lighthouse. (*Photo credit: US Coast Guard*)

Serial killer and career criminal Carl Panzram's mugshot at USP Leavenworth, 1929. (*Photo credit: USP Leavenworth photographic records, public domain.*)

life story, he describes his killings in major detail and how he callously dumped a good portion of his victims under the rocks of Execution Rocks.

In July 2009, Hector Barsali, a former Coast Guard keeper of the island in 1961, led the first public tour of Execution Rocks. During the tours, all participants were mandated to wear breathing masks as a safety measure. This precaution was necessary to protect against the hazards of peeling lead paint and mold prevalent in the keeper's quarters, which had remained uninhabited since 1978.

Even though there are no longer caretakers on the premises, visitors to the rock have reported apparitions, footsteps, and strange sounds.

Execution Rocks Lighthouse has been featured in various well-known paranormal television shows. If you are intrigued by its mysterious allure, you can consider taking a guided tour that departs from Port Washington, New York. The journey to Execution Rocks Lighthouse by boat typically lasts twenty to twenty-five minutes, offering a unique experience as you approach this historic site with such a horrific history.

4
FIORELLO DOLCE, HUNTINGTON, NEW YORK

Located on Wall Street in Huntington, tucked away off of Main Street, is everyone's favorite haunted bakery, Fiorello Dolce Patisserie. Owned by Gerard Fioravanti, the bakery is known for its exquisite desserts, made by some of the best pastry chefs in the business. It is also known for its poltergeist and ghostly activity. Reported activity has included knocks and bangs, moving knives on a magnetic strip that fall to the floor for no reason, anomalies, and mists captured on camera to name a few.

We were invited to come to the bakery and conduct a paranormal investigation. Intrigued, we happily obliged, grabbed our Gotham Paranormal equipment cases, and headed over to see if we could capture anything on our devices that would correlate to what Gerard had been experiencing. Each of our investigations turned up something new and different from the previous one. We were able to get continuous responses to ongoing question-and-answer sessions using our equipment. We were even able to capture a dog barking and a dog chain jingling which corresponded to Gerard's old dog, Figaro, who was always by his side and whose ongoing presence is always felt by Gerard. Investigations have captured giggles, equipment suddenly stopping and refusing to work for no reason, doors unlatching, dragging sounds, dog barking, and unexplainable odd taps and bangs hitting the microphone of the audio recorders.

The spirits that have always been present around Gerard at Fiorello Dolce and have never left his side. Being a sensitive and in tune with the spiritual realm, these entities have continuously made contact with him and his staff. Various spiritual mediums have made their way to the bakery multiple times, sharing their findings with Gerard and his staff. Among the spirits encountered, there have been family members, business partners, and even the ghost of a young man named Eddie, who tragically lost his life in an ancient narrow alley accessible through a door at the rear of the bakery. During one of our investigations, we did capture an image on camera of what appeared to possibly be the spirit of Eddie standing where he had died.

We researched the history of the location in which the bakery is located to see if anything, in particular, might be relatable to the activity. We also reached out to the Huntington Historical Society to see if they had information they could share with us. They were able to provide me with images of a few old maps of the area, but not much

Fiorello Dolce, Huntington, New York

Mist that formed during an investigation.

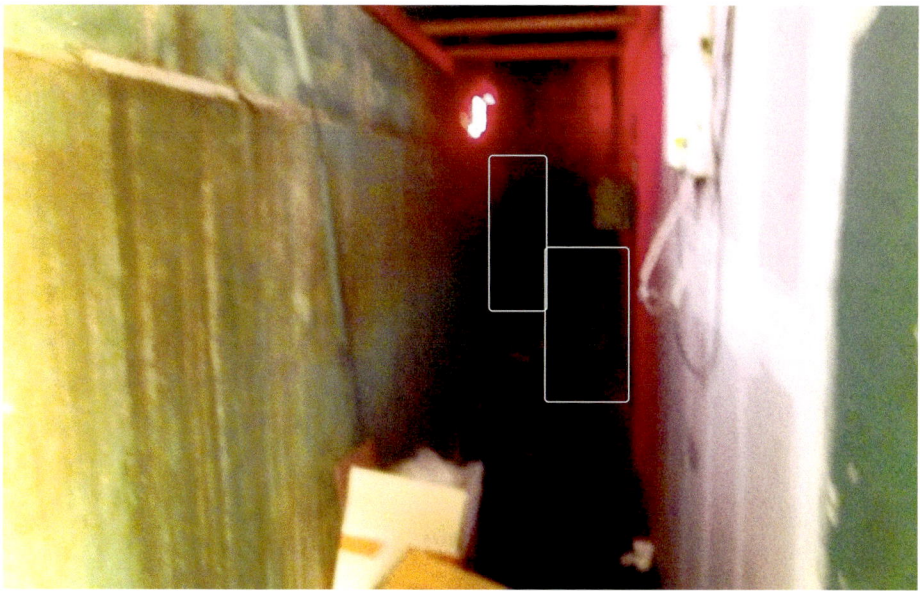

Possible image of Eddie on the right wearing a tee shirt.

in the way of history showed up for 57 Wall Street except that it was home to a cabinet/chair shop owned by Carman Smith in 1826. He was born in 1801 in the southern part of the Town of Huntington (known today as the Town of Babylon) and was a chair manufacturer. In 1843, Etna Fire Insurance Company occupied the space. We also were able to find that another cabinet maker and framer by the name of Elbert Walters moved his business to the same location in 1865.

Since tragic events can sometimes trigger paranormal activity, we searched for anything we could find in or near 57 Wall Street. A murder came up at the location of 55 Wall Street which is a bagel shop. Apparently, the husband, who was known to have violent outbursts, shot and killed his wife, shooting her twice in the head back in 2007. So far, the death of a young man named Eddie in the back alleyway is the only incident found to be related to that address.

There is a lot going on at Fiorello Dolce, and Gerard was happy to discuss all of it in his book, *The Baker's Ghost*, which is available in his shop, as well as on Amazon and Barnes & Noble. Treat yourself to the best pastries, cookies, and cakes on Long Island. Oh, and do not forget to say hello to all the spirits while you are there because they will be watching you!

5

FIRE ISLAND LIGHTHOUSE, FIRE ISLAND, NEW YORK

The Fire Island Lighthouse was initially built in 1826, standing at a height of only 74 feet. However, it was later replaced by a new lighthouse in 1858, which was constructed to be 168 feet tall, making it the tallest on Long Island. Even though the original foundation of the lighthouse can still be seen today, black and white bands were added to the cream-colored lighthouse in 1891. Its signal is visible for over 20–23 nautical miles. Besides serving as a navigational aid for sailors, the legends and tales surrounding the lighthouse have fascinated visitors and locals for many years.

The residence of the lighthouse keeper was completed in the year 1859 and was once connected to the lighthouse tower through a covered passageway. However, this passageway no longer exists. Both buildings are located on a terrace that stands about 15 feet high and have been constructed using stone. This stone was originally used in the construction of the lighthouse and the keeper's house, which was built in 1926.

There is a widespread belief that the Fire Island Lighthouse is haunted by the spirit of a former caretaker who took his own life in the 1800s. It is said that he was overwhelmed with grief after the death of his daughter, and his ghost is said to wander through the lighthouse.

During the 1800s, some construction work was being done on the lighthouse. At that time, Mr. Nathaniel Smith was the caretaker of the lighthouse. He was asked to live in a small shack near the lighthouse with his wife and daughter. Unfortunately, his daughter, who had already been suffering from breathing issues, fell sick due to the drafty and cold living conditions. To get her medical help, Mr. Smith called for a doctor. However, due to the lighthouse's remote location and rough waters, the physician took three long days to arrive at the lighthouse. Nathaniel Smith used to look out from the lighthouse every day to check if he could see the physician's boat coming. He did this for three days, as he felt helpless watching his daughter's health deteriorate with each passing day. Unfortunately, his daughter died before the physician arrived. Some stories suggest that Nathaniel's marriage could not survive the loss of their daughter, and he became increasingly despondent. Not having the strength to go on, he put a rope around his neck and hung himself inside the lighthouse. There have been reports of footsteps heard on the stairs of the lighthouse, along with the sound of a man moaning. Additionally,

Fire Island lighthouse.

Fire Island Lighthouse, Fire Island, New York

Fire Island lighthouse.

there have been sightings of a ghostly apparition who is sometimes seen holding a rope. It is speculated whether this could be the spirit of Nathaniel Smith.

Fire Island and its lighthouse have been featured in various movies and is a highly sought-after destination during the summer season. Some of the notable movies filmed there include *What Happens in Vegas* and *Men in Black II*, where it was transformed into a post office. The popular TV series *American Horror Story: NYC* also used Fire Island as one of its filming locations in 2022.

6

GOODY GARLICK AND THE LONG ISLAND WITCH TRIALS, EAST HAMPTON, NEW YORK

The seventeenth century was a challenging period for women, particularly if they were unmarried, widowed, or had enemies. The fear of witches spread like wildfire throughout America and Europe, putting everyone at risk. Accusations varied from simple gestures to unexplained livestock deaths and illnesses. Even natural occurrences like illnesses or deaths in the community could lead to accusations of witchcraft. The first witch trial in the U.S. is said to have taken place in 1645 in New England, but the witch hunts quickly expanded and persisted until the mid-1700s.

One of the most well-known incidents in New York history is the Long Island witch trial involving fifty-year-old Goody Garlick, which occurred in East Hampton in 1658. Elizabeth "Goody" Garlick, with "Goody" being a term for "Good wife," was the wife of Joshua Garlick. The couple were employed by Lion Gardiner, a former military officer, and a highly respected individual of that era. Lion Gardiner was the owner of Gardiner's Island, a property that remains in the possession of the Gardiner family to this very day.

Joshua Garlick had been employed at Lion Gardiner's island estate and was highly regarded as a dependable staff member. It is rumored that Lion Gardiner entrusted Joshua Garlick with transporting substantial amounts of his money for a purchase. Gardiner, who was born in England in 1599, served as an English army officer and a skilled engineer. His son, David, was born in 1636 and became the first white child born in Connecticut. His second daughter, Mary, was born in 1638, followed by his third daughter, Elizabeth, who was born on Gardiner's Island on September 14, 1641. Elizabeth was the first child born in New York State to parents of English descent. Gardiner's Island is situated in the Suffolk County region of Long Island, positioned in the twin forks between the Montauk Lighthouse and Orient Point.

Joshua Garlick was very well-liked throughout the community, but his wife, Elizabeth, was always felt to be "different" and was often shunned by the people of the town. She was always wandering off into the forest to collect herbs and according to town records, she was accused of performing satanic rituals in the woods.

In the fifteenth and sixteenth centuries, thousands of innocent women were killed throughout Europe because of a book entitled *The Malleus Maleficarum (The Hammer* of Witches). This book was written in 1486 for the Catholic church and was a book about "treaties on witchcraft." It was a guide that labeled witchcraft as heresy and dictated how to flush out, interrogate, and convict witches. The book advocated that torture and death were the only remedy for anyone suspected of witchcraft. The Americas then adopted this same practice.

Lion Gardiner had a sixteen-year-old daughter named Elizabeth Gardiner Howell. Right after giving birth, she began to have a fever and a cough that was progressively getting worse. She became delusional and had feverish dreams. She screamed hysterically that she was bewitched by a double-tongued woman who "pricks me with pins" and then coughed up a metal pin. She also screamed out that there was a black image around her feet, and she said it was Goody Garlick. She died the next morning. When the townsfolk heard news of this, some started to make accusations of their own accusing Goody Garlick of poisoning the milk of babies, causing children to become ill or die, and even causing harm and death to farm animals.

An inquiry board was assembled which consisted of three magistrates who, for three weeks, took the testimonies of all the citizens in the town. One of the main accusers was Goody Davis who accused Goody Garlick of causing the death of her child. She also accused her of causing an ox's leg to break, a man to go missing and die, and the death of a pig and its piglets during birth. Goody Garlick, herself, never took the stand to testify.

Lion Gardiner was said to be extremely uncomfortable with this trial. He had a strong admiration for the Garlicks and felt most of the accusations were really hearsay. He strongly felt that the only way for Goody Garlick to have a fair trial was to send her to Hartford, Connecticut, because they had more experience in trials like this. Goody Garlick was then escorted to Hartford by a very prominent settler named John Hand, Sr. who came to America from England in 1635 along with his wife, son, and father. He resided in Lynn, Massachusetts, first and then came to Southampton in March 1644. In 1649, he became one of the nine original founders of East Hampton, Long Island.

When the Garlicks arrived in Hartford, they were lucky to find that Connecticut had just received a new governor, a scholar, named John Winthrop, Jr., who was also said to be a healer. As luck would have it, he was not a very firm believer in the whole witchcraft hysteria and felt that Goody and her husband, Joshua, were accused simply because they were different from other people in the town. He felt that they were innocent and acquitted them of all charges. Elizabeth and Joshua Garlick returned to East Hampton and sued Goody Davis for defamation. Goody Davis subsequently died right after Goody Garlick's trial.

Elizabeth "Goody" Garlick and her husband were not the only ones to be tried for witchcraft in New York. In 1660, a woman who lived in Oyster Bay, Long Island, by the name of Mary Wright was accused of witchcraft and sent to Massachusetts for her trial.

In 1660, Mary Wright was suspected of having correspondence with the author of evil. Since the people felt there was no one competent enough to manage the case, she was sent to Massachusetts for trial. She was acquitted of the charges of witchcraft due to lack of evidence but was convicted of being a Quaker and banished from that jurisdiction.

In 1665, Ralph Hall and his wife were accused of taking the life of George Woods and his infant son by "wicked and detestable arts, commonly called witchcraft." It is said that George Woods and the infant both suddenly fell ill and died. There were no witnesses in court who were able to testify so they were acquitted of all charges and released.

In 1670, a widow by the name of Katherine Harrison ("Katharine Harryson") was also accused of witchcraft. She was the widow of John Harrison, who died in 1666, leaving a sizable estate. They had three daughters together, the oldest being Rebecca who was born on February 10, 1654. At some point before 1671, Rebecca became the wife of Josia Hunt, who was the son of Thomas Hunt and was named as the complainant against Katherine Harrison. The complaint stated that Katherine had caused a changing attitude in Thomas Hunt. She was accused of witchcraft, imprisoned, and indicted in May 1669. She was tried in October and found guilty by a jury but acquitted by the bench. Surrounding neighbors continuously complained to the town constable that she was a witch, who ordered her to leave. Katherine refused, but because of her good behavior, she was allowed to stay.

During the witch trial hysteria, many blamed the abnormal behaviors on the devil. In a 1976 report in the magazine *Science*, according to psychologist Linnda Caporael, the colonists ate rye, wheat, and other cereal grasses containing a type of fungus called ergot. It was later discovered that consuming this could cause muscle spasms, vomiting, delusions, and hallucinations—the very symptoms that were seen by the accusers in the witch trials.

7
Harbor Mist Restaurant, Cold Spring Harbor, New York

Nestled on the waters of Cold Spring Harbor, lies the beautiful and picturesque Harbor Mist Restaurant. Visitors and locals have frequented this fine dining establishment for years. Cold Spring Harbor has been reported to carry with it a slew of ghostly appearances and legends. Even the Harbor Mist is said to have its own resident ghosts that have been part of the restaurant for years.

According to books, website articles, and reports from those who have visited this area for years, the Harbor Mist has been said to harbor the spirits of several ghosts that roam throughout the establishment. Two of the ghosts were said to be there from when it was known as The Audsall Hotel, and the third was that of a woman who died a very strange death in the bathroom of the restaurant in the 1960s when it was known as The Whaler.

The history dates back to the 1800s when George Van Audsall purchased the inn and tavern. Back then, Cold Spring Harbor was a big whaling town, having an inn and tavern for sailors to come to drink and stay while they were in port would be deemed very profitable. During its time as an inn, it has been said that it also doubled as a brothel. Many of the women during that time were lonely with their men at sea for extended periods of time and money was scarce. One of the stories passed down over the years is that a woman whose husband was away at sea and took a job at the brothel. One day, her husband came to the inn to have a drink after his long voyage. While there, he found out that his wife had been working in the brothel upstairs. He immediately ran up to the bedrooms to find his wife and caught her with a man named Van Whether. In an instant rage, he murdered both of them on the spot. The ghosts of the two victims are said to roam the property to this day.

An article posted by The Patch dated May 25, 2011 states that a rather strange and unusual death was reported in a local newspaper in 1960 where a woman died in the ladies' room of the restaurant. The article is quoted as "a woman slipped in the ladies room and cut her throat on the ragged edge of a soap dish." The woman sadly died. I tried to track down the original article from 1960 but was unsuccessful. To this day, no one really knows exactly what happened in that bathroom that day.

Visitors and staff have reported apparitions and unexplainable occurrences. Sylvia Hughes and bartender Michelle Marchand have experienced a large amount of strange

Harbor Mist restaurant.

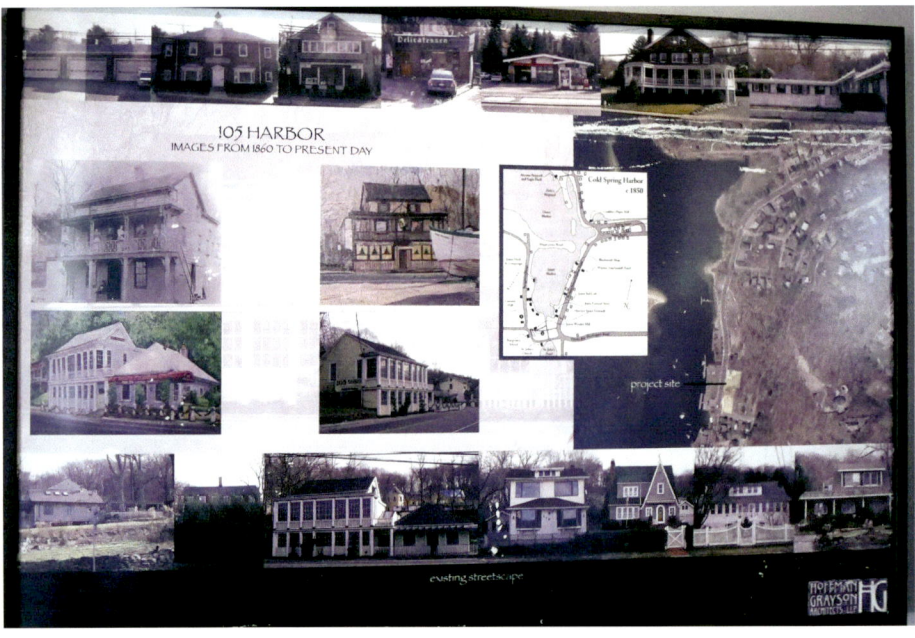

Images of Harbor Mist from 1860 to present day hanging in the reception area.

activity in the restaurant over the years. The owners, Barman and Michele Sharifi, also have had their fair share of strange and interesting occurrences as well. In the bar area, an image of a man was captured on one of the windows by Michelle which has been unable to be recreated. She has also witnessed a tremendous and unexplainable mist form in the bar area. As it was forming, she was trying to see what could have caused it to form but she could not find an explainable cause. There have also been reports of broken glasses and glasses shaking and clanking on their own in the racks. Again, with no explainable cause. Sylvia has had her share of spirit activity too. She witnessed what sounded like a complete ruckus in the ladies' room only to find that there was no one in there when going inside to see what was going on. She also heard someone in the bathroom stall shuffling their feet and banging, but again, no one was in there. Another strange occurrence is that the faucet turns on by itself whenever she arrives to the restaurant.

The entire staff is comfortable with their resident spirits, all except one. There was a server/busser who had just started to work there and was not familiar with the strange things that happened at the Harbor Mist. One day, he was upstairs (the site of the old brothel and double murder) and he saw an apparition of a lady in white. Stunned and petrified, he asked her what she wanted and what she was doing there. No one is quite sure what happened after that, but he bolted out the side door and never returned.

When we visited the restaurant, the staff was nothing but accommodating and truly a pleasure to talk with. While investing through some of the known hot spots where activity has been reported, you can surely feel a vibe that you are not alone. There has never really been any negative activity that has been reported and it seems that whatever is there, just really wants to be part of what's going on and enjoys being with people. We did not pick up on any type of negative energy at all while there. We also feel that there is some residual energy here as well. So, basically, there are two types of hauntings taking place here. One, is an intelligent haunting in which the spirit or spirits are aware of everything going on here and try to communicate. The other is a residual, where spirit energy does not communicate or interact with you at all. It just carries out a repetitive activity and it gets replayed over and over, similar to that of an old video that you rewind and play on a repetitive loop.

So, when you are driving through Cold Spring Harbor, be sure to stop by the Harbor Mist for a visit filled with great food, great people, and spirits. Maybe you will experience the presence of one of the resident ghosts—or maybe more.

The ladies' room inside the Harbor Mist where a mysterious death took place before it was the Harbor Mist.

Harbor Mist Restaurant, Cold Spring Harbor, New York

Above: The upstairs dining area that used to be a brothel in the 1800s when it was the Audsall Hotel.

Right: The main staircase to the upstairs dining room.

8
KATIE'S BAR OF SMITHTOWN, SMITHTOWN, NEW YORK

Upon entering Katie's Bar, it is common for visitors to experience a noticeable change in the atmosphere. There is a certain energy that seems to charge the space, a shift in the energy that is immediately noticeable from the very first step inside. Katie's is a place where the boundary between the past and the present feels remarkably thin and where the stories of old seem to live and breathe alongside the present. With each creaking floorboard and flickering light, visitors are reminded of the spirits that call this place home. The tragic events that unfolded within its walls over the years have become part of Katie's, creating an atmosphere that resonates with both mystery and sorrow. The bar is conveniently located on Main Street in Smithtown and resides right next to the Long Island Railroad which is easily and quickly accessible via the back parking lot.

Katie's has a tragic and significant past. In the 1900s, it was the location of the Trainor Hotel, but on December 5, 1909, the hotel burned down completely. There is no record of how many people lost their lives in the fire. However, after the destruction of the Trainor Hotel, new developments took place, and many establishments have operated on the property over the years.

One of the ghostly entities believed to inhabit Katie's Bar is a spirit named Charlie Klein, whose real name was actually Carl Klein. Charlie worked as a bartender in the Smithtown Hotel during the 1930s, which was located right next to where Katie's now stands. One night, when Federal agents visited the hotel, he served them beer, which, combined with the hotel's poor performance, caused him immense worry. Eventually, this led to an unclear and mysterious end to Charlie's story. On February 22, 1933, he went to his bedroom in the Smithtown Hotel, sat in a chair, put a revolver to his head, and pulled the trigger. He left behind his wife and family, who resided in Lindenhurst, while he ran the hotel.

Since that fateful incident, patrons and staff alike have reported eerie occurrences within the premises. Unexplainable sounds, apparitions, and inexplicable cold spots have been reported by those who have spent time within the bar. Brian Karpinnen, the owner, has had numerous experiences since owning the bar including a spirit that cradled him and protected him during a fall down the cement steps in the basement.

Gotham Paranormal has conducted numerous paranormal investigations at Katie's with a tremendous amount of findings over the years. EVPs (electronic voice

Katie's Bar of Smithtown, Smithtown, New York

Katie's of Smithtown.

NABBED FOR BEER SALE, KILLS SELF

Despondent over his arrest and release in $1,000 bail for selling beer last Saturday night, Carl Henry Klein, 69, committed suicide with a shotgun yesterday in the Smithtown Hotel, Smithtown Branch, L. I. The father of two children, Klein was arrested in a raid on the hotel Tuesday night. He was to have been arraigned in Federal Court, Brooklyn, March 8. His body was removed to his home at Lindenhurst.

HOTEL PROPRIETOR ENDS LIFE WITH GUN

Carl Klein, Smithtown Hotel Head, Found in Room.

Smithtown, Feb. 23.—Carl Henry Klein, 69, proprietor of the Smithtown Hotel, at Smithtown Branch, near here, shot and killed himself yesterday, according to the police. He was found in his bedroom on the second floor of the hostelry, seated upon a chair and it is thought by the police that he placed the muzzle of the shotgun against his head while seated and then managed to pull the trigger. The upper part of his head was blown off. He was dead when found.

Coroner William B. Gibson, who investigated the shooting, is of the opinion that Klein may have been worried over the visit of prohibition agents to the hotel last week. Business had been bad and it is believed by the police that Klein may have been worried over the prospects of his hotel being padlocked as a result of the visit by the Federal agents. He said nothing to any of the others in the place when he went to his room.

Klein leaves a wife and family at Lindenhurst, but had spent much of his time at Smithtown Branch conducting his hotel.

Above left: News report of Carl Klein's suicide. (*Photo credit: Daily News 2/23/1933*)

Above right: Another report of Carl Klein's suicide. (*Photo Credit: Brooklyn Times Union 2/23/33*)

phenomenon which are disembodied voices that are captured on recording devices) were captured in each room of the bar. During one investigation, several pieces of our equipment were missing from our equipment case. Oddly, we later found them halfway through the investigation in one of the upstairs booths inside coat pockets. Someone put them there and it was not us. We were the only ones in the building. The basement seems to be the source of a great portion of its paranormal activity. When you are in the basement, be sure to look at the floor. As you walk around the basement bar and get closer to the other end of the bar towards the pool table, you will see a change in the flooring which is referred to as the dividing line of where the Trainor Hotel once stood. The foundation is still there and there is a visible "line" of flooring from where the Trainor Hotel foundation stood and the extended area that was built around it. While in the basement taking EMF readings (electromagnetic field) around the bar and dividing line area, we noticed the KII meter (a device used to measure EMF) was pulsing high amounts, which we were attributing mostly to the electrical wiring, which was present at the time. KII meters are good indicators for obtaining quick EMF readings, but they are known to go off with certain types of interference. After a while, we noticed that the meter was pulsing a specific pattern. It was pulsing twelve times, then nine times, then five times, and it was doing it continuously till we realized that those numbers correlated to the date of the horrendous Trainor Hotel fire, which occurred on December 5, 1909, and not just a random pattern given off by the ice machine and other wiring. Cold spots and bouts of extreme heaviness were also noted in the basement.

On another occasion, while we had our cameras set up in the basement, we noticed something brief and unusual in the mirror near the pool table facing us. Upon looking through the images on our cameras, one image showed a young boy in period clothing wearing a scarf leaning on one of the poles in the basement. His image was captured in the mirror.

One of the most popular things experienced at Katie's is the breaking of glasses at the bar and the soda jerks coming out of their dispensers on their own which have also been captured on Brian's security cameras. Many have actually witnessed the glasses coming out of their holders and smashing to the ground, myself included. Keep in mind that these glasses are on high-up wall racks that have an actual lip on the rack, making one actually reach up and physically lift and take a glass out of the holder. As for the soda fountain jerks, they are pretty heavy, and for them to just lift themselves randomly out of the holders is definitely odd to witness. Many say it is the ghost of Charlie Klein.

We have investigated Katie's several times with different outcomes each and every time. It almost seems the spirits rotate and that some actually remember who they communicate with. With the use of mediums and other spiritual methods, Brian has tried very hard to remove the negative spirits that have occupied Katie's and have them move on. We had returned to Katie's after it had been shut down during the COVID-19 pandemic right before businesses were just starting to reopen once again. Brian had noticed something had been a bit "off" inside the bar and was curious as to what we could find. He wasn't wrong. The bar had a very lonely feel to it and a sense of overwhelming sadness, almost as if it was sad that it wasn't filled with its usual crowds and music. The spirits that were there with us almost didn't want us to leave, and it felt like they wanted us to tell them what was going on in the world. Those of us who have frequented Katie's over the years are well aware of the vibe it gives. It's like the spirits

Katie's Bar of Smithtown, Smithtown, New York

Right: Boy wearing a scarf captured in the basement mirror of Katie's Bar.

Below: Main bar at Katie's.

of Katie's know that its guests care and worry about them, and they know when they return. The spirits are also very protective of Brian, the owner.

Katie's has been featured on numerous shows over the years and is considered to be one of the most haunted locations on Long Island. It is also one of the best venues that hosts many of the greatest popular bands performing throughout the week. With great drinks, great music, special events, an outdoor patio in the summer, and warm hospitality, visitors are always welcome and guaranteed a great time. Oh, and don't forget to make a toast to Charlie before you leave.

9
Terry-Ketcham Inn, Center Moriches, New York

The historic Terry-Ketcham Inn is located in the Center Moriches part of the Town of Brookhaven in Suffolk County. The inn dates back to the Revolutionary War era and has served as a residence, tea house, restaurant, and boarding house over the years.

However, in 1989, a fire damaged the dining room. That same year, the Ketcham Inn Foundation was established and purchased the property. After years of neglect, the foundation proceeded with a major restoration project to restore the inn to its historic colonial appearance, and on March 9, 1992, the Terry-Ketcham Inn was added to The National Register of Historic Places.

The oldest section of the inn dates back to the 1600s, a time when the area was still unsettled. Initially, it served as an inn and a small settlement cottage. In 1698, Samuel Terrill, a blacksmith, purchased the inn from Jacob Doughty. In 1714, Sarah Scudder Conkling, the widow of John Conkling of Southold, bought the inn from Terrill. When her husband died in 1705, he left Sarah and their two sons, John and Henry, a considerable sum of money, as well as the property in Southold. The property was later sold to John Havens, Jr. When John Havens, Sr. passed away, a significant amount of money was distributed to his sons, including John, Jr., Benjamin, and Henry.

During the Revolutionary War, Benjamin Havens managed the tavern within the inn. He had close ties to the Culper Spy Ring, as his wife, Abigail Strong, was the sister of Selah Strong. Selah Strong was related to the chief spy of the Culper Spy Ring, Abraham Woodhull, through his mother, Suzanna Thompson. Benjamin Havens assisted the cause by spying on British troops.

In 1791, Havens sold the inn to William Terry who continued to run it as an inn, naming it "Terry's Inn." It was reported that James Madison and Thomas Jefferson stayed at the inn while traveling to visit William Floyd at his estate. The descendants of Terry sold the inn to Andrew Ketcham of Huntington around 1851/1852. The Ketcham family owned the inn until 1912.

The remarkable restoration efforts have beautifully restored the Ketcham Inn. Visitors can feel transported back in time to the era when stagecoaches would pull up front to let guests off to stay at the inn, drink in the tavern, and even dance in the ballroom. The goal for the Ketcham Inn is to become a living museum and farm, where everyone can

Photo of the Terry-Ketcham Inn. (*photo credit: KetchamInnFoundation.org*)

visit and experience a glimpse of life in the eighteenth and nineteenth centuries. In the 1800s, a young girl lost her life inside the inn after being severely burned. People have claimed to see apparitions of the young girl and hear her voice throughout the inn.

The Foundation's property features a Book Barn located inside the barn and carriage house. The Book Barn operates for most of the year, except during the coldest winter months. The Foundation's website provides information on the dates and times of operation. Additionally, the website lists various fundraisers held throughout the year, and tours are also available.

10

Lake Ronkonkoma, Ronkonkoma, New York

One of the most ancient tales originating from Long Island, dating back to the 1600s, recounts the story of Tuskawanta, the Indian princess. She fell deeply in love with a woodcutter named Hugh Birdsall, residing on the opposite side of the lake. Each day, spanning seven long years, she penned heartfelt letters on bark pieces, setting them afloat down the river to reach her beloved. Tuskawanta's father, the esteemed chief of the Setauket tribe, sternly opposed their bond, as relationships beyond the tribe were strictly prohibited. Heartbroken and burdened with immense sorrow, she navigated her boat to the lake's core and tragically ended her own life by piercing her heart. According to the legend, due to her profound grief, it is believed that she claims the life of one man annually.

There are several different versions of this tale that have circulated throughout the years when discussing the legend of "The Lady of the Lake." Some versions of the legend suggest that Tuskawanta, consumed by despair and grief, took her own life by plunging a blade into her heart, her anguished spirit forever haunting the waters of the lake she so dearly loved. Others recount a tale of star-crossed lovers, torn apart by the cruel hand of destiny as Hugh met a tragic end, driving Tuskawanta to follow him into the depths of the lake, where they would find solace in an eternal embrace. Another version suggests that her beloved took his own life, leading her to tragically follow suit by drowning in the lake upon hearing the news. In a different variation, her lover discovered her lifeless body in a canoe drifting along the lake, prompting him to leap in after her, and both were never seen again. Despite their devotion, fate conspired against Tuskawanta and Hugh, leading to a tragic end that would echo through the ages.

There are some mysterious features of a lake that have people wondering what secrets it holds. One of the most intriguing things about this lake is that it rises and falls without any apparent cause from the weather or precipitation. Many have tried to find an explanation for this phenomenon, but so far, no one has been able to offer a reasonable one. Additionally, when people drown in the lake, their bodies are often never found. Some believe that the lake might be bottomless, while others suggest that there may be deep cavernous tunnels that transport the bodies elsewhere into larger bodies of water. Author Michael R. Ebert conducted his extensive research and writings

Lake Ronkonkoma.

shedding light on the shadowy secrets that Lake Ronkonkoma holds. His work, titled *The Curse of Lake Ronkonkoma*, delves deep into the heart of the legend, unraveling its mysteries and exploring the enduring legacy of the Lady of the Lake. His interest in the curse of Lake Ronkonkoma was sparked by the death of a classmate in the 1990s who unfortunately had drowned in the lake.

On the northside of the lake, one can see the beautifully carved wooden statue of the Lady of the Lake, Tuskawanta. The statue was created by artist, Todd Arnett, who worked on the 32-foot-tall statue for approximately four years.

Although the legend of the Lady of the Lake has been a strong one for years and something many ponder when they visit Lake Ronkonkoma if there really is a Lady of the Lake. As visitors gaze upon the serene waters of Lake Ronkonkoma, they cannot help but ponder that age-old question. Perhaps the answer lies hidden within the whispers of the wind and the gentle lapping of the waves, waiting to be discovered by those brave enough to seek the truth.

The lake's dark reputation as a watery grave for the unfortunate souls claimed by its depths only adds to its mystique. Countless tales of drowning tragedies spanning the centuries have fueled speculation about the lake's true nature. Some believe that hidden currents or underwater caverns may be responsible for the mysterious disappearances, while others attribute the phenomena to the restless spirit of Tuskawanta, exacting her annual toll on the lives of unsuspecting men.

LAKEVIEW CEMETERY, PATCHOGUE, NEW YORK

In the quiet old town of Patchogue, Long Island, stands one of the oldest cemeteries known as Lakeview Cemetery. The land on which the cemetery stands has seen its share of historical, prominent people in history, revolutionary war heroes, murder victims, those who perished in sunken ships, and numerous others. The cemetery runs along Main Street and Waverly Avenue in the western section of Patchogue. Lakeview Cemetery itself is actually a combination of five cemeteries which include Episcopal, Gerard, Rice, Waverly, and Lakeview Cemetery.

The Congregational Church, the original church building, was built in 1794 on the corner of Main Street and Waverly Avenue, along the edge of the cemetery. The Episcopal, Gerard, and Waverly sections of Lakeview Cemetery contain the oldest graves dating back to the 1700s, and it is felt that those cemetery sections were placed there because of the church at that time.

One of the most famous stories of those buried in Lakeview Cemetery is that of the tragic sinking of the 163-foot schooner *Louis V. Place*, which sunk off of Fire Island in February 1895. According to the article published in *The Sun* on February 11, 1985, the schooner was sailing from Baltimore to New York carrying a cargo of coal when a sudden gale storm hit as they approached Long Island. On board was a crew of eight; the captain and seven crew members. As the intensity of the storm was getting stronger, and temperatures rapidly dropping, the boat began to fill with water too quickly for the men to keep up. They tended to their posts and struggled with all their might to hold on in the icy conditions. Out of the eight-member captain and crew, only two were rescued, while the remaining six perished. When visiting Lakeview Cemetery, you can find the burial plots of the *Louis V. Place* as soon as you enter, located on the right side. Eight plots were erected, but only four of the deceased are actually buried there: Charles Allen, August Olson, Gustave Jaiby, and Fritz O. Mard. There is also a headstone for Captain Squires, but he is not buried there. His body is buried in Southold, Long Island.

Also laid to eternal rest is the crew of the *Nahum Chapin*, which sunk in 1897 along the coast of Patchogue. Their graves are directly alongside the crew of the *Louis V. Place*.

Located directly across from the sailors, you can find the graves of the Smith sisters: Charlotte Goldsmith Smith Keech, Betsey Ann Smith Roberts, Augusta Josephine Smith

Dedication memorial to the *Louis V. Place*.

The graves of the sailors of the *Louis V. Place* facing the graves of the Smith sisters.

Lakeview Cemetery, Patchogue, New York

Graves of the sailors and memorial stones honoring the *Louis V. Place* and the *Nahum Chapin*.

Dedication memorial to the *Nahum Chapin*.

Weeks, and Ruth Newey Smith. These very wealthy women were known to be the wealthiest in Patchogue. With all of them being seamstresses, they took their sewing talents to Manhattan and eventually opened up their own cloak business which proved to be extremely successful. As their wealth and popularity grew, they became local philanthropists, and their kindness and generosity became unmatched.

The four sisters provided the graves and burials for the sailors of the *Louis V. Place*. It is said that one of the sisters, Augusta, was so terrified of being buried alive that she put in her will that she not be buried until five days after her death to ensure she would not be buried alive by mistake. It is said that in Augusta's will she wanted her body to be kept warm, placed in a warm room, and her clothing was to remain on. There was to be no use of ice or embalming fluid anywhere on her body.

Located several feet behind the sailor's graves, towards the fence, is the gravesite of little seven-year-old Helen Tiernan, who suffered a horribly tragic death, being brutally murdered at the hands of her own mother. The seven-year-old's mother, also named Helen, was a single mother raising her two children: Helen, who was seven years old, and her little brother, Jimmy, who was five years old. Helen had fallen in love with the man she had been dating. However, he did not want to share a home with young children and was preparing to leave her. When she found out about his intentions to leave, she decided to rid herself of her children. She took the children on a trip out to Long Island near Montauk Highway where she found a forest area off Yaphank Avenue. She then immediately attacked them both using the blunted end of a hatchet causing both children to fall to the ground, dazed. According to little Helen's younger brother, Jimmy, the mother proceeded to strangle her daughter and then cut her throat. She also cut the throat of little Jimmy immediately after attacking his sister, hitting him with the hatchet as well. Thinking they were both dead, she poured gasoline over them, setting them on fire, and left them in the wooded area. As soon as she was done, she walked back to the train station and boarded the next train out to New York City. Helen Tiernan was found and arrested for her horrendous crime, and it is said that little Jimmy was sent to an orphanage and later adopted, but there is no further information available. Little Helen's spirit is said to wander through the cemetery to this day.

Not too far from the grave of little Helen Tiernan are the graves of Elizabeth Oakes Smith, who was a very famous nineteenth-century poet, and her husband, Seba Smith, who was a famous political satirist, editor, and author.

In the 1800s, the cemetery rested on top of a small hill which was often referred to as "Blood Hill." Various books and articles researched indicate that it possibly got its name from all the drunken bloody fights that took place there. Some speculate that the fights were so bad that the streets were running with blood. On top of that hill stood "Blood Mansion." Research done by others indicates that the house on Blood Hill was once owned by Brewster Woodhull, a possible relative of Revolutionary War hero Nathanial Woodhull. Records indicate that Brewster Woodhull sold the house to Seba and Elizabeth Smith in 1860. Seba and Elizabeth worked diligently to renovate the house and because they loved the surrounding willow trees so much, they named it "The Willows." Not too long after they bought the home, Seba Smith sadly died in the house in 1868. Elizabeth eventually moved out of the house in 1870.

Multiple families were said to have moved into the mansion but none of them lasted long. They claimed that there was something strange going on in the mansion as well

Lakeview Cemetery, Patchogue, New York

Gravesite of the Smith sisters.

Gravesite of the Smith sisters facing the graves of the sailors.

Lakeview Cemetery, Patchogue, New York

Above: Gravesite of Helen Tiernan.

Right: Close-up of the tombstone of Helen Tiernan.

Grave of Elizabeth Oakes Smith.

Grave of Seba Smith.

as throughout the cemetery. Reports were coming in from several of the most popular newspapers of that time that indicated there were numerous reports of strange sounds and ghostly sightings. Some residents of the area felt the hauntings could possibly be due to the reported slave pen that was in the basement of the mansion.

Residents of the town claimed this cemetery had originally been haunted as a result of having been the site of a house that contained a "slave pen" in the corner of its basement that was used to hold and punish any disobedient slave. Some claimed that the bodies of those slaves who did not survive their punishments were dragged and buried in unmarked graves in the cemetery. In 1893, the house was destroyed by fire. It is said that the people of the town just watched it burn to the ground because of its evil reputation.

Another building that no longer stands on the property is the old Harts Tavern. After the Revolutionary War, George Washington was known for stopping there while touring Long Island. The tavern was reported as standing on the site, which is located in the cemetery, near Main Street. In the 1920s, a plaque was placed there by the Daughters of the American Revolution, marking the approximate location. There are some online researchers who claim that Harts Tavern, as well as the Oakes-Smith House, and the house on Blood Hill are all the same house. There are also claims that the underlying foundation of the haunted house was filled in after the fire and is still there, buried

Lakeview Cemetery.

below an area of depressed land, which can be seen to the right once you enter the cemetery.

Over the years, people who have visited the cemetery claim to have heard the sounds of crying, as well as apparitions, and even the sounds of someone whistling. There have also been reports of some seeing the apparition of a young girl roaming through the cemetery. There have been reports of whistling that are said to have been heard near the graves of those who perished on the *Louis V. Place*. This is rather interesting since sailors would whistle while on their ships as a means of communicating with each other.

Lakeview Cemetery is one of the oldest cemeteries on Long Island. For quite a few years, it had become overgrown and in need of care, but thanks to Steve Gill's leadership and the countless hours of the Lakeview Restoration Committee, it has been given tremendous attention with restoration efforts and ongoing maintenance. A tremendous amount of care has gone into caring for Lakeview Cemetery and it is open for visitors to see. As always, please be respectful; no trespassing. More information can be found on their website as well as their hours for visiting.

12

Montauk Lighthouse, Montauk, New York

The Montauk Lighthouse, perched proudly atop Montauk Point, stands as a sentinel of maritime history, bearing witness to tales of triumph and tragedy that have unfolded upon the tumultuous seas below. With its storied past, the lighthouse has become not only a beacon of warning for ships navigating the treacherous waters surrounding Long Island Sound but also a focal point for legends and ghostly lore, with one particularly haunting figure at its center: Abigail.

Perched upon an elevated expanse known as Turtle Hill, the Montauk Lighthouse overlooks a stretch of coastline that has long been feared by sailors for its rocky shoals and treacherous currents. Originally named "Womponamon" by the Montauk tribe, meaning "to the east," this elevated land served as a gathering place for tribal councils, marked by fires lit atop its summit. Throughout history, Montauk Point has been synonymous with danger for seafarers, its unforgiving terrain claiming countless vessels and lives. During the American Revolution, the British soldiers used it as an elevated location and would set fires on Turtle Hill that would be used to guide their ships which blockaded Long Island Sound.

Montauk Point was one of the most dangerous areas for any ship to sail near the 100-mile shoreline of Long Island Sound. Its treacherous rock-filled waters and sandbars destroyed numerous vessels along its path. In 1792, Congress bought the land on which a lighthouse was to be built to prevent further loss of ships and trade. The lighthouse would warn all passing vessels of the treacherous rocks surrounding Montauk Point. Approximately three to four years later, President George Washington authorized the construction.

Heavy blocks of sandstone were hauled up to the top of Turtle Hill with an order from New York bricklayer John McComb to begin digging the 13-foot-deep foundation. The base of the lighthouse was to have a 28-foot diameter with walls that were 9 feet deep. The top of the 80-foot tower was to have walls that were 3 feet thick. A two-story keeper's house was also built along with a storage house to keep the oil needed for the beacon light.

One of the most interesting stories about the lighthouse includes the ghost of Abigail, who is said to have haunted the lighthouse since 1811. Apparently, there are

Montauk Lighthouse, Montauk, New York

Montauk Point lighthouse.

Phone used to communicate with the top of the tower.

The light at the top of the lighthouse tower.

View from one of the lighthouse tower windows.

two different versions of the story: one is a classic love story, and the other involves a shipwreck. So, who is Abigail?

Abigail Olsen is said to haunt the lighthouse and many people who visit it have claimed to see and hear her. Henry Osmers, the Montauk Lighthouse historian, shares a story in one of his interviews that says that seventeen-year-old Abigail was the daughter of one of the workers who helped to renovate the lighthouse in 1860. Abigail began dating another worker whom her father did not approve of and put an end to their relationship. It is said that Abigail died of a broken heart and returned to the lighthouse in search of her love. The other story about Abigail is that of a ship that sank during a huge winter storm on Christmas Day off the coast of Montauk in 1811. It is said that Abigail was a passenger on that ship. When the ship sank, it was said that she made it to the shore and was rescued. She was carried into the lighthouse where, unfortunately, she died.

Portrait of Abigail which hangs inside the lighthouse.

There was not much documentation that would enable one to find a woman named Abigail in love with a lighthouse worker in 1811 or 1860, and researching that particular story turned up nothing but dead ends. That said, I did find a few details that were well-documented on the shipwreck of the *Traveler* at Montauk Point during that time.

On December 23, 1881, a vessel called *Traveler* was approaching the waters of Long Island Sound when a huge blizzard began to hit. Temperatures dropped drastically and treacherously high, forceful winds rocked the ship over the high waves of the rocky waters. The ship was commanded by Capt. Davis Conklin who was married to Zerviah Hand from East Hampton/Montauk. The crew of three, along with two passengers and the captain, became lost in Long Island Sound, the storm that was known as "The Christmas Storm" or "The Great Christmas Blizzard." The next day, the shipwrecked vessel was found at Eaton's Neck.

There were six people aboard the vessel: Captain Davis was found frozen to death. The two passengers, Miss Sally Mulford, who was visiting South Hampton along with her brother, were both frozen to death. Lastly, the three crew members, Clothier Baker of Sag Harbor, who survived; Abraham Payne of Amagansett, who also survived; and Ebenezer Buck, the ship's cook, who froze to death.

There was no record of anyone named Abigail on board the ship. I even tried searching through all the shipwrecks of 1811, and none had a documented passenger named Abigail Olsen. I even tried searching for any captain of a shipwrecked vessel in 1881 with the last name of Olson, Olsen, or Oelson but still came up empty.

Hopefully, one day we will be able to learn more about Abigail. In the meantime, visitors to the lighthouse have reported hearing strange noises, seeing things moving and many feel as if someone is tugging on their clothing. A beautiful painting of Abigail hangs inside the lighthouse for visitors to see which has been reported to be seen moving. Furniture moving on their own in the middle of the night has also been reported. Some claim to have seen the image of Abigail climbing the lighthouse steps or strolling on the grounds.

Montauk Lighthouse holds tours and various events throughout the year. Their website is always frequently updated. Be sure to visit Abigail's portrait that hangs inside the lighthouse and don't forget to be on the lookout for her climbing the steps of the lighthouse.

Montauk Lighthouse, Montauk, New York

Steps inside the lighthouse.

View from inside the lighthouse.

13

Montauk Manor, Montauk, New York

The quaint and peaceful landscaping on which the Montauk Manor now sits was a site of tumultuous activities during the 1600s to 1800s. It has been widely known that you do not disrupt graves, especially Native American burial grounds, without suffering any type of consequences. A manuscript memoranda of the deceased John Lyon Gardiner, who was known to be well versed in the history of eastern Long Island, indicated that in 1663, a war prevailed between the Pequots and the Narragansett tribes. The Block Indians sided with the Narragansett's and the Montaukers with the former. They set out in the war canoes under a full moon. As the Montaukers arrived, they were ambushed with one party slaughtering them and another party destroying their canoes. Only two Montaukers escaped and were able to notify their friends and family of the bad news. The Narragansett tribe took the Sachem of the Montaukers and ordered him to walk in his bare feet on a large flat rock heated with burning fire. His feet burned to coal while singing his death song until he fell ending the last of the wars. As if this wasn't enough, they were all hit with a severe case of smallpox, killing them in great numbers. They were not allowed to come anywhere near the town while infected and if they did, they would pay a penalty or be whipped.

Those tragic events could have been just enough to set up a future of strange paranormal events for anyone or anything on those grounds. Enter the Montauk Manor.

Standing over four stories high, Montauk Manor is the largest hotel in Suffolk County, Long Island. It was built on the former site of an Indian fort and overlooks Fort Pond Bay. Montauk was once home to the Montauk Indian tribe who played an important role in the council of the original thirteen other Long Island tribes.

Montauk Manor was the dream of entrepreneur, Cal Fisher, who was tremendously successful in developing all the major resort areas in Miami Beach. He wanted to bring the same exclusive resort style to Long Island and did just that when he built the Montauk Manor during the Roaring '20s. The manor was to be designed in a Tudor Revival style and was designed by the same architects who were well known for their work on the elegant Waldorf Astoria in New York City. The manor officially opened its doors in 1927 and attracted wealthy, high-society guests from near and far to bask in its elegance and luxury.

Montauk Manor in the 1920s. (*Photo credit: Montauk Historical Postcards, Montauk Library Archives*)

With over 200 rooms set on over 10,000 acres of land, Montauk Manor offered everything one could ask for. It had luxurious gardens, a golf course, spacious ballrooms, and even an airfield for the elitists who could come and go in their private planes. To put it short and sweet, it was a playground for the wealthy.

Unfortunately, the Great Depression of the 1930s proved to be detrimental to the Montauk Manor and caused a major impact on its success. Cal Fisher and his development company lost just about everything. Others tried to revive it and try to make money back on it, but all attempts failed, and many went bankrupt in the process. The manor had changed many hands over the years, and it wasn't really until the 1980s when major changes were made, and the manor began to see a very welcome and lucrative change.

The manor was built on Fort Hill, where the Montaukett Indian "fort," or rather "stockade," once stood in the seventeenth century and was used to protect women and children. This large plot of land referred to as Meeting Rock was used as a cemetery for Native Americans, and another section of that land was used for tribal meetings.

An article from the Montauk Library indicates that in the 1980s, the locals of Montauk said that some of the Montaukett graves had been desecrated by the development of the Montauk Manor. In 1983, Robert Cooper, a descendant of the Montaukett tribe, along with other members of the public, sounded off further excavations of the land. This led to the town purchasing the property and Robert Cooper became head of the Fort Hill Advisory Board for Fort Hill Cemetery.

Montauk Manor advertisement flyers.

Montauk Manor. (*Photo credit: Beyond My Ken, Wikimedia Creative Commons*)

A white quartz boulder referred to as Council Rock, used to be present at the site of all tribal meetings that included representatives of all thirteen Long Island tribes. It was moved from the foot of Fort Hill to the cemetery where it now remains. According to Robert Cooper, the cemetery's location on Fort Hill was spiritually significant, and he was quoted as saying, "Open to the four winds, the setting and rising suns, and high above the sea. It is absolutely suited for what it has been and will be used for."

Over the years, people have reported hearing and seeing many unexplainable events taking place inside Montauk Manor. Doors opening and closing on their own have been reported. The sound of drums has also frequently been heard in the graveyard and near the manor itself. Shadows have been reported and some have even claimed to hear the sound of chanting. One guest claimed to find herself levitating a few feet above her bed and was moved to another floor. Guests and staff have reported seeing a Native American Indian chief dressed in traditional Native American attire. He is seen on the fourth floor and seems to take watch over the guests of the manor.

The Montauk Manor is definitely a must-see. Between its elegant splendor and haunted history, it offers something for everyone to explore and enjoy.

14
Mount Misery and Sweet Hollow Road, Melville, New York

Two of the most sought-after locations for those interested in horror, mystery, and the paranormal have to be Mount Misery and Sweet Hollow Road. These two locations have attracted paranormal enthusiasts for years. Located in the wooded area of Huntington, New York, they have become a must-see location for decades. The stories they hold, which have become local legends, are full of tragic events and ghostly sightings.

Mount Misery is a very dark and desolate road. The road runs from the intersection of Chichester Road/Hartman Hill Road and leads to a dead end. Years ago, the land in this location was noted to be very hilly and rocky, causing farmers to have major damage to their wagons and weeks. The road was said to be treacherous and just a plain miserable road to travel on, hence the name Mount Misery Road. Over the years, the road seemed to become even more treacherous to automobiles since the road itself was very narrow and very dark and winding. Local teenagers trying to see if the local lore is true, would drive down the road and turn off their headlights to achieve total darkness to see if they run into any of the so-called horrors that haunt the area.

The legends that have been passed down through the years are quite interesting, and every so often, there seems to be another change in the stories or new ones added. One of the most popular stories is the legend of the police officer who will pull you over if you are caught driving down the road. Once he pulls over the car, he asks the driver for their license and registration and begins to issue a ticket. Nothing strange really about that except when he turns to walk towards his police car, the back of his head is missing. He then instantly vanishes.

Next, we have the demon dog. The legend of the demon dog is that this rather huge black dog with deep red eyes hides alongside the road, waiting for cars to come his way. It is said that anyone who sees the dog will meet a quick and untimely death. Along with the demon dog, there is also a dog that runs around digging holes and then walks around on his hind legs. Oh, and let's not forget the ghost horse that gallops through the woods and suddenly disappears from sight.

Adding to the road's mystique is the legend of a long-forgotten mental institution, rumored to have stood nearby in the 1800s. According to local whispers, a female patient with white hair and a white gown set fire to the institution using matches,

Mount Misery and Sweet Hollow Road, Melville, New York

Mount Misery Road.

reducing it to ash and ember. Though the asylum itself has long since crumbled into obscurity, its tragic history lives on in the form of spectral apparitions said to wander the surrounding woods. Some say the stone steps to the hospital are still there, buried in the ground, but no one to date has ever found them.

No spooky story would be complete without a lady in white. Legend says that a woman named Mary was hit by a car and killed. She is said to roam up and down the road or jump in front of cars to try and hitch a ride with whoever passes. Another story of the Lady in White is that of a spirit that forms from a mist who roams around looking for her long-lost love. Could this be the same woman in white who died in the mental institution? No one really knows, but the legends continue, and many with several different versions. There is also another Mary and the story of Mary's Grave who was said to be murdered. She was very young, and the tombstone that sits upon her grave is engraved with an angel that is said to cry real tears.

Some who have driven down Mount Misery Road have also noted other anomalies. Some claim that they experienced electrical problems with their cars and devices such as cell phones, and some claim to have experienced engine trouble.

Sweet Hollow Road, which is nearby, has its own ghostly legends. The area got its name Sweet Hollow because of the overabundance of sweet honey in the 1800s. Eventually, the town name was changed to Melville, but Sweet Hollow Road kept its name.

One of the most popular legends is that of the bridge overpass. It is said that at night you can catch a quick glimpse of several teenagers who hung themselves off the bridge. It is said if you honk your car horn three times, you will catch a glimpse of them hanging off the bridge. Another story is that a school bus full of children lost control during a storm and fell off the bridge without any survivors. It is said that if you put your car in neutral, the children will push your car. This story was tested many times by visitors to Sweet Hollow Road who all noted that there was a slight incline in the road that would cause the car to move. Another version is that a camp counselor was crazed and killed the children of his camp. There is also another story of driving down Sweet Hollow Road at midnight to see if their cars would shut off.

Another sighting, slightly different from your usual spooky ghost story, is a report made by a New York DJ who reportedly saw a UFO while at Mount Misery. Author John A. Keel tells a chilling story of strange happenings at Mount Misery in his book *The Mothman Prophecies*. These documented accounts involve UFOs, men in black, predictions made by outer-worldly beings to those who witnessed UFO activity, and more. In the 1960s, a Long Island DJ by the name of Jaye Paro reportedly saw a UFO at Mount Misery. The area had been a hot spot for UFO sightings which were witnessed by many. Jaye Paro along with all the others who witnessed a UFO sighting, all reported that they were visited by men in black who wanted to hear more about their experiences. When Paro reported what had happened on her radio show, she began receiving strange and threatening phone calls that invited her to meet back at the site; she refused. The callers all had metallic-like voices and demanded her to "meet at the Mount."

On June 11, 1967, a very strange woman showed up at the WBAB studio to talk to Jaye Paro. The woman was about 6 feet tall with large glassy eyes and was wearing some kind of feather-covered costume. She was wheezing and having difficulty breathing. As author Keel writes, the woman said, "I am Princess Moon Owl. I am from another

The overpass.

planet. I came here by flying saucer." DJ Paro immediately started the tape recorder, and the princess happily obliged to provide a thirty-minute interview talking about life on planet Ceres in the asteroid belt. UFO researchers claim that Cerians had a problem with severe body odor. Jaye Paro stated that the smell of rotten eggs was overpowering but continued on with the interview. Princess Moon Owl told her that she was "seven oongots" which meant 350 earth years old.

After the interview, several calls came into the author, John A. Keel, claiming to be Princess Moon Owl; however, in his opinion, they clearly were not from her. Once DJ Jaye Paro aired the interview, Princess Moon Owl began to contact all the prominent Long Island UFO enthusiasts. She knew exactly who to call even if their numbers were unlisted. It got to the point that anyone who witnessed a UFO sighting knew they would be visited by Princess Moon Owl.

Once people heard the broadcasted interview with Princess Moon Owl, everyone started to flock to Mount Misery to see if they could capture a UFO or strange being. One story in particular was about a young woman named Jane who took a drive with her boyfriend, Richard, to Mount Misery. When they arrived, he stopped the car, stating that he suddenly felt ill. Moments later, he fell unconscious. At that same moment, a terrified Jane witnessed a brilliant beam of light shooting out from the woods next to the road. She became dazzled by the light and fell back, unable to move. The next thing they both knew, they were driving on Old County Road at the bottom of Mount Misery, having no clue what had just happened or how they got there. A few days later, Jane received a strange phone call at home with the caller's voice sounding very metallic-like. The caller instructed her to go to the nearby library and look for a particular book on Indian history and go to page 42. When she went the next day, the library was deserted except for one librarian who looked like she was from the 1940s. It seemed that the woman was expecting her and as Jane approached, she was handed the book from under the desk. Jane took the book to a table and quickly turned to page 42 as instructed.

The following is taken from *The Mothman Prophecies: A True Story* by author John A. Keel and is what Jane described to the author in the book:

"You won't believe this," she told me, "but the print became smaller and smaller, then larger and larger. It changed into a message and I can remember every word of it. 'Good morning, friend,' it began. 'You have been selected for many reasons. One is that you are advanced in autosuggestion. Through this science, we will make contact. I have messages concerning Earth and its people. The time is set. Fear not … I am a friend. For reasons best known to ourselves you must make your contacts known to one reliable person. To break this code is to break contact. Proof shall be given. Notes must be kept of the suggestion state. Be in peace. [signed] A Pal.' The print became very small again, and then the normal text reappeared." As soon as Jane left the library she became quite ill and vomited several times during the next two days. She approached Miss Paro with her story and was advised to get in touch with me. Her experience on the Mount, her phone call, and the remark about "autosuggestion" all stirred my interest. In those days, none of the UFO enthusiasts knew anything about these factors, and a hoax seemed very unlikely. And, unknown to Miss Paro and Jane, I was in touch with a distant contactee who was communicating with "Apholes." The signature "A Pal" seemed close enough to Apholes to take seriously. I suspected that Jane had been programmed for a set of special experiences, and I kept in constant touch with her in the months that followed, maintaining an extensive record of her experiences.

The book continues with numerous experiences and strange occurrences, visits from men in black, and beings from beyond this world. The above is just a small snippet of what the author incurred during his research and interviews. There have been so many ghostly stories about Mount Misery and Sweet Hollow Road, but this is the very first time I ever heard about UFO sightings there. This is just another reason, and probably scarier than the original folklore, to be wary of visiting alone—and at night.

15

OHEKA CASTLE, COLD SPRING HARBOR, NEW YORK

Located in Cold Spring Harbor, Oheka Castle is the largest mansion on Long Island's Gold Coast. This immense residence, designed in Victorian-style architecture, dates back to the early 1900s. It sits on over 443 acres of land and was built around 1915 to 1919 by Otto Hermann Khan. His daughter, Maud, was the very first bride to be wed at Oheka Castle in 1919. How did something so magnificent and beautiful make its way to Long Island? Let's take a look.

German-born financier Otto Hermann Khan had become extremely popular managing the financial accounts for some of the largest railroads in the nation. These included the Chicago and Eastern Illinois Railroad, the Missouri Pacific Railroad, and the Baltimore-Ohio Railroad. With the incredible wealth he gained, he decided to build a country-style manor in Morristown, New Jersey. The newly constructed manor was named Cedar Court and opened in 1905. Unfortunately, it was completely destroyed by a fire shortly after.

After searching for another location to build, Otto Khan purchased over 440 acres of land in Cold Spring Harbor for the sum of $1 million. Afraid of another repeat fire, he took extra care in the construction of this home, constructing it out of steel and concrete, making it the very first fireproof residential building. By the time construction was completed, the Khan family had invested over $11 million into their new home complete with a dining room, library, thirty-nine fireplaces, and over 127 separate rooms. Also, inside was a magnificent ballroom. Lastly, no castle would be complete without an eighteen-hole golf course and set of tennis courts.

Researching the history of Oheka Castle revealed some very interesting facts. Oheka's original name was derived from Mr. Kahn's, Otto Hermann Kahn. Another interesting fact is that legend states that Mr. Kahn inspired Mr. Monopoly in the board game Monopoly, which makes total sense since he was a financier of all those railroads.

The castle served the Kahn family well over the years until Otto Khan's death due to a heart attack in 1934. Oheka was sold to the City of New York and used by the Department of Sanitation as a retreat for its workers and a government training school for Merchant Marine radio operators. In 1948, it was used by the Eastern Military Academy as part of its campus. When the academy went bankrupt, Oheka laid dormant

The Otto Khan Estate in 1915. (*Photo credit: Wikimedia Creative Commons*)

The gardens at Oheka Castle. (*Photo credit: www.flickr.com/photos/cynicalplanet/*)

and abandoned for a good number of years. Unfortunately, vandals took the opportunity to set numerous fires to the abandoned building over a five-year span.

The castle was eventually purchased by Gary Melius in the 1980s, who did a complete renovation in an attempt to restore the mansion as close as possible to the interior's original appearance. A new roof was needed and the same company that created the original roof in the early 1900s, Rising & Nelson Slate Co. was the same company used to supply over 4,000 roof slates needed to repair the roof. In addition to the roof, the gardens were completely updated and over 220 missing windows and doors were replaced inside the mansion. A non-profit, Friends of Oheka, to help keep and protect Oheka Castle in all its splendor. The updating and renovations also included the addition of The Oheka Bar and Restaurant as well as The Terrace Room.

Many famous people have visited Oheka over the years, including Charlie Chaplin, Orson Welles, Harpo Marx of the Marx Brothers, and composer George Gershwin, to name a few. Oheka has also been used in many famous movies and television productions such as *Citizen Kane, The Great Gatsby* (2000 film), *The Emperors Club, Royal Pains, What Happens in Vegas, It's a Funny Kind of Story, As the World Turns, America's Castles, Great American Railroad Journey* (BBC), *Lifestyles of the Rich & Famous, Madam Secretary, Madoff, Mega Mansions, Succession, Treasures of New*

Oheka Castle, Huntington, Long Island, NY. (*Photo credit: Oheka Castle, Creative Commons*)

York, Taylor Swift video "Blank Space," *Real Housewives of New York City* season 12 reunion, and Mr. Beast.

Visitors and guests of the hotel have reported various paranormal claims such as footsteps, disembodied voices, and doors opening and closing by themselves. Some have reported ghostly images in the mirrors and unexplainable cold breezes with no cause.

Oheka Castle is well known for its extravagance and beauty and all the guest rooms and suites share the most beautiful views of the estate, offering each guest a luxurious and extravagant experience. Book a stay and enjoy a luxurious getaway. Don't forget to bring a camera. Maybe you will be one of the lucky ones to get the full experience and capture one of Oheka's resident ghosts. Mansion tours are offered with further information posted on their website.

16

Old Burying Ground and Fort Golgotha, Huntington, New York

Located on Main Street in Huntington lies the Old Burying Ground, which is located right behind the Soldiers and Sailors Memorial Building. It is also referred to as Old Burial Hill, Old Burying Ground, and Ancient Burial Ground. The burial ground was established in the seventeenth century, shortly after the town was founded in 1653. Many of the earliest graves were made of slate and sandstone. Buried here are three of the town's founders, Ketchum, Sammis, and Conklin. The earliest death recorded in Huntington was of Jeffrey Este, who died on January 4, 1657, and it is presumed that he is buried in Old Burial Ground. The last burial that took place was that of Russell F. Sammis, who died on May 2, 1957.

During the American Revolution, British troops occupied the area from September 1, 1776, to March 1783. They secured this site to keep a watchful eye on Huntington Harbor. This was a very tumultuous time for the people of the town. British Colonel Benjamin Thompson ("Count Rumford") ordered that the Old First Presbyterian Church be dismantled and a fort to be constructed. The patriots had secretly removed the 556-lb. church bell from the tower and hid it in the home of John Wicks. Unfortunately, it was discovered by the British and seized to use on British warships, including the brigs *Swan* and *Rhinoceros*.

The timbers from the church were used in the construction of the fort which was named Fort Golgotha. The people of the town were forced to aid in the construction and preparation of the burial ground for the fort. Fort Golgotha was completed in fifteen days. There was massive desecration of the burial ground by the cold and callous Col. Thompson (later known as Count Rumford). The British barracks were built on top of the bones of the earliest graves and were full of profanity and debauchery. They cut down 114 apple and pear trees, destroyed 9,500 chestnut rails, and stripped wood from locals' homes and barns to use to build the fort. Town records indicate that one hundred tombstones were dug up and removed. The tombstones were used as part of the construction of the fort, such as tables, fireplaces, floors, and even ovens. It is said that they used to bake bread on the tombstones, and many of them saw the epitaphs of their friends and loved ones baked onto the crust of the "tombstone bread."

The third minister of the church, Reverand Ebenezer Prime, was buried in the Old Burial Ground in 1779. The cold-hearted Col. Thompson made sure that the fort's exit was placed directly in front of Reverand Prime's grave so that he could walk upon it each time he entered and exited the fort.

Huntington's old burying ground.

Old burying ground.

Old Burying Ground in Huntington, Old Burying Ground

Burying ground.

Grave of Ebenezer Prime.

Four months after the construction of Fort Golgotha and the desecration of the burial ground, the British troops evacuated the area and left Huntington. The townspeople tore down Fort Golgotha leaving the foundation still in the ground. They began to work on building their new church, Old First Church, which still stands today. The original church bell was located aboard the ship *Rhinoceros* which was docked in New York City; however, it was cracked and unusable. It was eventually sent to be recast in Connecticut before it could be used until 1967. It currently remains on display with the words "The Town Endures" engraved on its interior as a reminder of that dark period in time.

The cemetery is easily accessible and located behind the Soldiers and Sailors Memorial Building. A metal chain-link gate is accessible from the parking lot alongside the memorial. Although we could not find the exact spot where Fort Golgotha once stood, there were a few areas where small clearings were noted that could have possibly been the location. Several trees with huge bases are still on the grounds, clearly having been standing there during the revolutionary times. The grounds are extremely rocky and hilly and many of the older tombstones were difficult to read after being weathered over the years. People visiting the cemetery claim to have heard voices and experienced unexplainable cold spots. Some have reported seeing white figures at night walking through the cemetery. Others have reported seeing apparitions that quickly come and go. There is also a memorial near the parking lot for Nathan Hale.

Huntington Town Historian Robert C. Hughes provides a detailed map and listing of all those buried in the cemetery at longislandgenealogy.com/OldHuntington.pdf. If you plan on visiting the Old Burial Ground in Huntington, this map and detailed list will be very helpful in locating all the graves.

Cemetery.

Burying ground.

Sailors and Soldiers' Memorial Building.

Nathan Hale Memorial.

Plaque on the Nathan Hale Memorial.

Old Burying Ground in Huntington, Old Burying Ground

The Nathan Hale Memorial

17

POPPER THE POLTERGEIST, SEAFORD, NEW YORK

Just about all of Long Island has been built on Native American land. Many of the older stories and legends about paranormal activity usually end up being chalked up to a location being built on an ancient burial ground and that the native spirits who once owned the land were angry. There are some locations where much of that information from the early years is not properly documented. It definitely gives one something to think about when presented with a case of strange and forceful activity witnessed by people around the globe that simply has no explanation whatsoever. The story of little Jimmy Hermann and his family is that case.

The Hermann family lived in the quiet town of Seaford. They were your average family next door who found themselves thrust into one of the most well-known cases of poltergeist activity ever documented. The case was referred to as Popper the Poltergeist because it would pop the tops off of all the bottles in the house. Back in 1958, the Hermann family lived on Redwood Path in Seaford. It was your basic '50s home that was built in 1953. It had three bedrooms, a bathroom, a kitchen, a small dining room, a living room, and a basement. The basement contained a playroom for the children as well as a utility room.

The Hermann family, consisting of James and his wife, Lucille, along with their two children, Lucille, age thirteen, and James, age twelve, moved into their cozy home on Redwood Path, seeking a peaceful life in the suburbs. Marie Murtha, Mr. Hermann's cousin, was a frequent visitor to their Seaford home. The family had lived in the house for a few years when their lives would take an unexpected turn.

On February 3, 1958, the Hermann family went about their usual day. The kids went to school, Mr. Hermann went to work, and Lucille Herrman was preparing dinner and waiting for the kids to return from school. It was just an ordinary day in the family's life. However, this ordinary day would swiftly transform into a swirl of chaos and confusion. As soon as Lucille's children returned home from school and entered the kitchen, a sudden and unexplainable phenomenon unfolded before their eyes. Bottles began to tremble and burst, their contents exploding into a frenzy of liquid chaos.

It was initially thought that the activity was contained to just the kitchen; however, the mayhem soon spread like wildfire throughout the Herrmann household. With each

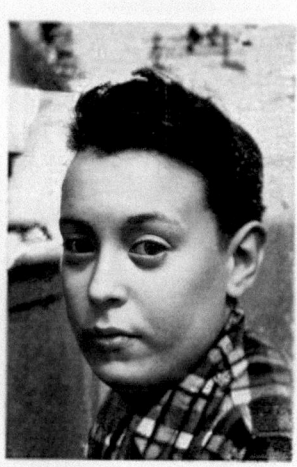

PRINCIPAL CHARACTERS are James Herrmann, his wife Lucille and son James, 12. Most but not all of the flights have occurred near young James.

The James Hermann family. (*Photo credit: House of Flying Objects, LIFE Magazine, March 17, 1958*)

step, they found themselves surrounded by the aftermath of continuous bottle explosions everywhere they went. From the pantry to the living room, from the basement to the bedrooms, no corner of their home was spared from the explosive onslaught. Shampoo bottles in the bathroom, cleaning supplies stored in the basement, and even medicinal remedies tucked away in the medicine cabinets were exploding, rupturing with alarming force.

Mrs. Hermann, a nurse by trade, urgently called her husband, who was working in New York City for Air France. She did her best to describe the unsettling incident to him. Both of them were at a loss trying to comprehend what had transpired and what might have triggered the bottles to open and shatter. Since it seemed to have stopped at the time of the call and everything else seemed under control, Mr. Hermann decided to just finish out his workday and return home at his usual time.

Thinking it might have been just a chemical reaction of some sort or a change in temperature that caused the strange reaction, they assumed it was just a one-time weird anomaly. However, three days later, the same thing happened again. On the following night, the bottles popped open again for good reason. James Hermann paid close attention this time and tried to figure out if his son was behind the strange occurrences scheming some sort of prank. He suspected that Jimmy might have rigged the bottles with some sort of science experiment, such as carbonated capsules, to make them explode after a certain amount of time. This would not be the case. On February 9, more bottles began to shake and pop open without Jimmy even being near them, leaving the Hermann family completely baffled. Mr. Hermann became increasingly upset that this could still be a prank, so he confronted Jimmy while he was brushing his teeth in the bathroom. Suddenly, a medication container slid across the countertop into the sink, followed by a shampoo bottle that fell to the floor.

The Hermanns kept a bottle of holy water in their room that they also noticed would unexpectedly open multiple times on its own. They also had a statue of the Virgin Mary on their dresser, which was hurled about 12 feet and collided with the mirror.

All of this upset and frightened the Hermanns and left them at a complete loss. Not knowing what to do next, Mr. Hermann called the Nassau County Police and tried to explain what was happening and ask them to send help. The police, thinking it was a prank, had a hard time taking him seriously. After much convincing, they finally sent someone to the house to check it out.

Officer James Hughes, the officer assigned to the task, approached the house with hesitation, convinced that the entire situation was nothing but a prank. Upon reaching the Hermann's residence, the family inside welcomed him to delve into the peculiar occurrences. Suddenly, a series of bottles unexpectedly burst open, their caps flying off in all directions, with many of them seemingly targeting Officer Hughes directly. Startled by the bizarre turn of events, Hughes promptly returned to the police station to document a detailed report, urging for a thorough investigation to be conducted.

Detective Joseph Tozzi was assigned to investigate the Hermann case. He stayed at the Hermann home to try and personally experience the strange occurrences reported there and watched the family very closely. Despite his presence, the activity continued, with bottles popping open everywhere and ceramic figurines being thrown past his head. As a result, Detective Tozzi was left completely dumbfounded and at a complete loss as to what exactly was going on.

Being Catholic, the Hermann family reached out to Father William McLeod, who was a priest at the Church of St. William the Abbott, for assistance in removing any harmful presence that could be lingering in their house and conduct a blessing, thinking that would help. Even after Father McLeod conducted a thorough blessing using holy water in every room, the strange occurrences continued and this time, it seemed to get worse.

Detective Tozzi worked tirelessly on the case, leaving no stone unturned in the search for the cause. They looked into various possibilities such as radio waves, sonic booms, and jets flying overhead, but none of them proved to be the cause. The poltergeist activity showed no signs of stopping and was only getting worse. In one instance, a 100-pound statue of a horse was thrown across the basement floor all by itself, while he and Jimmy began walking down the basement steps. Building inspectors, fire marshals, and the Long Island Lighting Company were all called in to inspect, but they found nothing wrong and could not determine the cause.

Everyone was at a complete loss. The strange occurrences had been going on relentlessly for a full two weeks and news of the haunting quickly spread like wildfire across Seaford. Referred to as "Popper the Poltergeist" by local media, the mysterious entity became a mix of fascination and terror for the neighborhood. TV crews stationed themselves outside the Hermann house, eager to capture a glimpse of the unexplainable events that had captivated the town. Reluctantly thrust into the limelight, the Hermanns found themselves bombarded by journalists and well-meaning neighbors offering uninvited advice on how to manage their ghostly visitor. All sorts of people with outlandish ideas began showing up at their doorstep, each claiming to have the solution. Some religious individuals began praying on their lawn, convinced that demons had taken over the house or that the Hermanns were involved in dark magic rituals. The chaos became unbearable, and the family simply wanted nothing more than to escape from it all. Despite their pleas for privacy and understanding, they were drowned out by the noise of speculation and sensationalism. News outlets, radio stations, and newspapers all clamored for their story. Even prestigious publications like Time and Life magazines expressed interest in the so-called poltergeist. The Hermann family found themselves engulfed by the media and a constant stream of onlookers, receiving endless calls from various sources, some offering solutions while others accused them of dark magic practices and summoning evil forces into their home.

A woman from Revere, Massachusetts, who had been following the story reached out to the Hermanns. She told them that she had a very similar experience in her home with her furniture moving on its own and that it was found to be coming from a severe draft in her fireplace. She claimed that once they capped it off, the furniture instantly stopped moving. The Hermann family attempted to do the same, but the poltergeist activity persisted, almost immediately after the workers completed the capping, catapulting a porcelain figurine that was thrown 12 feet and ended up being captured on a television broadcast.

Almost three weeks after the activity started, it appeared to be getting increasingly more powerful and violent. It started with bottles popping open, and now heavy statues, porcelain and ceramic figurines, and heavy sugar bowls were being hurled about. Flashbulbs belonging to a photographer were seen levitating and smashing against the wall. Detective Tozzi remained with the Hermanns. He was becoming increasingly concerned about the violent activity taking place and he feared for their safety. On February 24, a bookcase in Jimmy's room was thrown to the ground, and his record player was thrown 15 feet across the room. A globe was also thrown out of Jimmy's room and hurled down the hall, almost hitting Detective Tozzi.

The Hermann family was experiencing some troubling occurrences, and they were in dire need of help. Despite the detectives' reluctance to attribute the strange happenings to paranormal activity, they were running out of logical explanations and were willing to try anything at this point. The team at Duke University's Parapsychology Lab had been tracking the case, and on February 26, Dr. J. Gaither Pratt, an assistant of Dr. J. B. Rhine, was called in to assess the Hermanns' home. He believed that one of the family members was responsible for the disturbances, while other researchers concluded that the house was haunted by a poltergeist, a mischievous ghost known for causing chaos and making a lot of noise.

Dr. Pratt and the researchers at Duke University had observed a correlation between adolescent children and poltergeist activity. This phenomenon has become known in the paranormal community as an occurrence that centers around young teens going through puberty. For some reason, the presence of an adolescent is often associated with this type of paranormal activity. These teens are usually unaware that they are responsible for the phenomena. In the case of the Hermann family, Jimmy, a twelve-year-old boy, was present for almost all of the incidents that occurred and never once felt that it was he who was causing all the activity to happen.

Dr. Pratt dedicated a significant amount of time to Jimmy. They worked on homework assignments together, enjoyed games, and engaged in conversations. Throughout the entire visit, there was no hint of anything unusual happening. Dr. Pratt enlisted the help of his colleague, William G. Roll, and they proceeded to interview and spend time with all the family members. The interviews revealed that everyone was truly deeply affected

Gothic Long Island

Parapsychologist Joseph Gaither Pratt observing James Hermann's son of the Seaford poltergeist case. (*Photo credit: Robert Wallace, Public domain, via Wikimedia Commons*)

by the challenging circumstances they had been facing and strongly felt that this was in no way any type of hoax.

The atmosphere was calm until March 2 when a dish unexpectedly flew out of the cabinet and shattered on the floor. Jimmy's night table was also overturned, and a bookcase in the basement did a complete 360-degree flip. This was a clear indication that Popper, the mischievous poltergeist, was back—or never actually left. On the evening of March 10, there were popping sounds coming from the basement. Dr. Pratt and his colleague immediately went down to see what was going on, and they found a bleach bottle still in its box but with its cap missing.

And then, just as mysteriously as it had begun, the activity ceased without warning and objects everywhere in the home remained undisturbed. It seemed that Popper the Poltergeist had vanished, hopefully for good, as inexplicably as it had appeared, leaving behind a bewildered family and a community grappling with unanswered questions.

Following the eerie occurrences, the Hermann family decided to avoid attention and not revisit the traumatic events that took place inside their old house. Despite the lack of a definite explanation for the strange happenings, the story of Popper the Poltergeist remains a baffling puzzle, reminding us of the endless mysteries that exist beyond human understanding.

The family has since moved away from the home in Seaford and there have been no reports whatsoever of unusual or unexplainable activity ever occurring again since that time of the Hermann's experience. Could all the activity that had taken place in

Popper the Poltergeist, Seaford, New York

It was alleged that a bookcase had fallen over in the basement at James Hermann's house. (*Photo credit: Public Domain, Wikimedia Commons*)

the home possibly have been caused unsuspectedly by Jimmy? It is a known fact in the paranormal community that children and adolescent teens are more susceptible to strange and unusual activity but the cause of this has never truly been determined.

Although this is not a location that could be visited, I included it here as it is a classic story that just about every investigator on Long Island has known. It is definitely one of the most interesting cases of poltergeist activity ever documented.

18
RAYNHAM HALL, OYSTER BAY, NEW YORK

Nestled in the heart of Oyster Bay, Long Island, stands Raynham Hall. This historic house dates back to the eighteenth century, and played a pivotal role during the American Revolution, serving as a haven for British soldiers and later as a meeting place for American patriots. The house's most infamous resident, Robert Townsend, was part of the Culper Spy Ring, which provided critical intelligence to General George Washington.

The Townsend's were a highly respected family in Oyster Bay. Samuel Townsend, a Quaker and successful merchant, earned his livelihood by bringing in goods such as tea, spices, wine, rum, and pottery on his fleet of four ships. These vessels journeyed to the Caribbean, Europe, and South America. In 1738, Samuel Townsend acquired the land and property that we now recognize as Raynham Hall, where he resided with his wife, Sarah, and their eight children. Over time, the residence underwent substantial renovations and was later inherited by his son in the 1940s.

During the American Revolution, Townsend's home became the headquarters for the British under Lt. Col. John Graves Simcoe for a period of six months. One of John Simcoe's frequent visitors was the British Maj. John Andre. It has been said that Samuel Townsend's daughter, Sally, overheard the two men discussing Benedict Arnold's plot to surrender the fort at West Point to the British. Sally's brother, Robert Townsend, was in a secret group called the Culper Spy Ring and she immediately alerted him of the plan. Robert Townsend passed the information to George Washington and the plot failed. Major John Andre was captured and hanged, but Benedict Arnold escaped by boat and was never captured.

The Culper Spy Ring was an American spy ring that was created to provide George Washington with information about the British troops. Appointed by George Washington in November 1778, Maj. Benjamin Tallmadge was put in charge of creating the spy ring in New York City which was the site of British headquarters. Maj. Tallmadge's code name used in the spy ring was John Bolton, Abraham Woodhull was Samuel Culper, Sr., and Robert Townsend's was Samuel Culper, Jr. Maj. Tallmadge took great care in choosing his informants, and he chose only those he trusted most. Many were friends he had made at school which included Caleb Brewster, Austin Roe, Anna

The front entrance to Raynham Hall.

Raynham Hall landmark sign.

Above left: Robert Townsend.

Above right: Samuel Townsend.

The other side of Raynham Hall showing the additions to the home.

Raynham Hall, Oyster Bay, New York

Lt. Col. John Simcoe.

Strong, and Abraham Woodhull. Robert Townsend, another trusted informant who posed as a merchant, also worked as a journalist which enabled him to gather important information from the British while at gatherings. For the safety and protection of all the spies, Maj. Tallmadge devised a numerical code system that consisted of 763 numbers to be used instead of names and locations. George Washington's code number was 711, and Robert Townsend's spy name, Samuel Culper Jr., was code number 723. Also in the spy ring was a woman whose identity was never revealed. She was known as "355." To this day, although there is some speculation, it is still not known who she was. Coded messages from George Washington to Maj. Tallmadge were delivered by Austin Roe and taken to Abraham Woodhull's farm and hidden for him to retrieve at a safe time. Anna Strong, who lived on a farm next to Abraham Woodhull, also took part in the spy ring by hanging a black petticoat on the clothesline. This system would be a signal to Caleb Brewster that it was safe to retrieve the documents and deliver them to Maj. Tallmadge. Andre's last visit to Raynham Hall was shortly before his capture and execution by hanging as a spy. His bedroom was upstairs, and the British officers remained downstairs on the ground floor and occupied most of the front rooms.

Townsend had three daughters. The middle one was Sarah, often referred to as "Sally" by those closest to her. Sally was eighteen years old when she met Simcoe, who was twenty-seven years old and looking for a wife. Legend has it that Simcoe was completely smitten with Sarah and the two flirted with each other continuously. Located inside Raynham Hall is the very first documented Valentine in the United States that was given to "Sally" (Sarah) Townsend on February 14, 1779, by officer John Simcoe. It is on display inside Raynham Hall and reads as follows:

Culper Spy Ring.

NAME	ALIAS	CODE #	POSITION	BORN	DIED
George Washington	None	711	Spymaster	1732 Virginia	1799 Mt. Vernon, VA
Benjamin Tallmadge	John Bolton	721	Chief of Intelligence	1754 Setauket	1835 Litchfield, CT
Abraham Woodhull	Samuel Culper Senior	722	Head Spy	1750 Setauket	1826 Setauket, NY
Robert Townsend	Samuel Culper Junior	723	NYC Spy	1753 Oyster Bay	1838 Oyster Bay, NY
Austin Roe	None	724	Courier, LI - NYC	1748 Setauket	1830 Patchogue, NY
Caleb Brewster	None	725	Whaleboat Captain	1747 Setauket	1827 Black Rock, CT
Anna (Nancy) Smith Strong	None	None	Spy Support	1740 Setauket	1812 Setauket, NY
Jonas Hawkins	None	None	Courier, Jan. -- June 1779	1752 Stony Brook	1817 Stony Brook, NY

List of alias names and their code numbers. (*Photo credit: allthingslibertydotcom*)

Raynham Hall, Oyster Bay, New York

Fairest Maid, where all is fair,
Beauty's pride and Nature's care;
To you my heart I must resign,
O choose me for your Valentine!
Love, Mighty God! Thou know'st full well,
Where all thy Mother's graces dwell,
Where they inhabit and combine
To fix thy power with spells divine;
Thou know'st what powerful magick lies
Within the round of Sarah's eyes,
Or darted thence like lightning fires,
And Heaven's own joys around inspires;
Thou know'st my heart will always prove
The shrine of pure unchanging love!
Say; awful God! Since to thy throne
Two ways that lead are only known—
Here gay Variety presides,
And many a youthful circle guides
Through paths where lilies, roses sweet,
Bloom and decay beneath their feet;
Here constancy with sober mien
Regardless of the flowery Scene
With Myrtle crowned that never fades,
In silence seeks the Cypress Shades,
Or fixed near Contemplation's cell,
Chief with the Muses loves to dwell,
Leads those who inward feel and burn
And often clasp the abandon'd urn,—
Say, awful God! Did'st thou not prove
My heart was formed for Constant love?
Thou saw'st me once on every plain
To Delia pour the artless strain—
Thou wept'sd her death and bad'st me change
My happier days no more to range
O'er hill, o'er dale, in sweet Employ,
Of singing Delia, Nature's joy;
Thou bad'st me change the pastoral scene
Forget my Crook; with haughty mien
To raise the iron Spear of War,
Victim of Grief and deep Despair:
Say, must I all my joys forego
And still maintain this outward show?
Say, shall this breast that's pained to feel
Be ever clad in horrid steel?
Nor swell with other joys than those
Of conquest o'er unworthy foes?

> *Shall no fair maid with equal fire*
> *Awake the flames of soft desire:*
> *My bosom born, for transport, burn*
> *And raise my thoughts from Delia's urn?*
> *"Fond Youth," the God of Love replies,*
> *"Your answer take from Sarah's eyes."*

Along with the poem, Simcoe drew a small sketch of their both initials inside two hearts, shot by Cupid's arrow. On a pane of glass preserved from Sarah's bedroom, there is an etched message on the glass to Sarah from John Graves Simcoe. It reads: "The adorable Miss Sally Sarah Townsend." Unfortunately for Simcoe, Sarah had backed away from furthering the relationship. She never married and died at the age of eighty, a single woman.

In 1914, Julia Weeks Cole, with the help of her sister, Sallie Townsend Coles Halstead, purchased Raynham Hall and used it as a tearoom. In 1933, Miss Coles deeded the house to the Oyster Bay Daughters of the American Revolution, who maintained the house during the Depression and eventually was given the house by Miss Cole in 1941. Approximately six years later, upkeep became too much for the Daughters of the American Revolution, and they offered the building to the Town of Oyster Bay which took possession of it in 1947. In the 1950s, the town and advisory committee made the decision to restore the home back to as it was in the eighteenth century.

Over the years there have been numerous claims of paranormal activity experienced inside Raynham Hall. According to an article in the *Farmingdale Post*, dated October 27, 1938, written by Julia Coles, the paranormal activity just might be the spirit of Maj. John Andre.

When Raynham Hall was once operating as a tearoom, an overnight guest was given the same room that was occupied by British Revolutionary spy Maj. John Andre when he used to visit Col. John Simcoe. The following morning, the guest told the hostess that she had seen a man on a white horse enter her bedroom. Many believe this is the ghost of Maj. John Andre. It is said that when this apparition is seen, a death in the family is soon to be reported. Oddly, the same apparition has also been reported in the original Townsend Home in England and the reported drowning death of the earl of Craven, whose wife was a Townsend descendant.

The lady who was renting out Raynham Hall and using it as a tearoom at the time, said unexplainable noises would often be heard and felt like invisible people were walking up and down the stairs. Her cook at the time, was so frightened that she gave her notice. Other servants also had seen and heard ghosts but felt that if they didn't bother them, the ghosts wouldn't bother them either and would leave them be.

Miss Coles' sister, Sarah Townsend Halsted, described to her what had happened to her cousin, Mrs. Batchelder, when she brought her small Pekinese dog with her to attend a meeting at the Daughters of the American Revolution. Mrs. Batchelder brought the dog upstairs but noticed that the dog "gave every indication of sheer terror and couldn't be dragged past the spot." They returned a year later, to the day, and the same exact incident occurred again.

Miss Cole's sister also reports seeing the ghost of Robert Townsend. While she was in the library, she heard footsteps in the upstairs hall. When she looked out, she saw the

Raynham Hall, Oyster Bay, New York

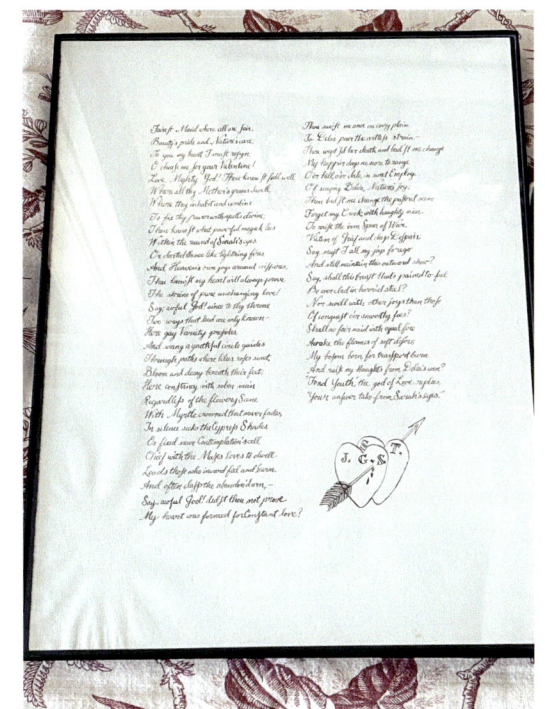

Right: Valentine written by John Simcoe to Sarah Townsend.

Below: Hallway into the dining room.

Bedroom in Raynham Hall.

Upper floor of Raynham Hall.

The Brown Lady, Raynham Hall, England. (*Photo credit: Hubert C. Provand e Indre Shira, CC BY-SA 4.0 creativecommons.org/licenses/by-sa/4.0, via Wikimedia Commons*)

form of a little, bent old man walking slowly down the hall. When she walked out to get a closer look, he disappeared. She said he fit the exact description of Robert Townsend. On another occasion, her sister went to Raynham Hall to pick up some books that were in a cupboard underneath the bookcases. The cupboard was never known to be locked, but on this occasion, it was. They tried repeatedly to unlock the cupboard, but no matter how hard they tried, they could not get it open. The next morning, it opened easily and was mysteriously unlocked.

Miss Cole reports that her sister had witnessed numerous apparitions ever since she was a young child. She once saw what they refer to as the Gray Lady walk into a clothing wardrobe and disappear. The woman was said to be tall and wore a tight-fitting gray gown. She walked across the bedroom, opened the door to the wardrobe, entered, and disappeared. Their grandfather, who lived in Albany, was the owner of the wardrobe, but no one knows where he got it from or what happened to it.

Oddly, after that experience, it was reported that the earl of Townsend met her on the stairway one day in the other Raynham Hall located in England. When he asked his mother who she was, he was told there were no guests staying in the house at that time. It is presumed that this lady was the Lady in Brown, the sister of Sir Robert Walpole, whose name was Dorothy. She was married to the second Viscount Townsend. There is a very famous photograph that was published in *Life* magazine on January 4, 1937, showing the woman on the stairs. Many felt it was the image of the Lady in Brown was Dorothy. The photo's authenticity was attested at the time the negative was developed by a respected panel of London chemists who had a representative present at the time the photo was being developed.

There have been many who say that Raynham Hall in Oyster Bay is haunted and many claim to have seen apparitions of spirits wearing clothing very similar to what would have been worn during the time of the Culper Spy Ring. Also reported are doors opening and closing on their own and sounds of footsteps when no one else is in the home. The sound of disembodied voices has also been heard. When Gotham Paranormal investigated there, we captured many unexplainable voices on our audio recorders known as electronic voice phenomenon or EVPs for short. One, in particular, was an EVP that clearly said "Sarah." Learning more about the detailed history of Raynham Hall over the years makes one wonder: could these be the spirits of the officers and/or the staff during that time? We will never truly know for sure, but it is definitely quite possible, especially when there is no other explanation.

Raynham Hall is a very strong advocate for historical preservation and was listed on the National Register of Historic Places in 1974. Their ongoing work with organizations and individuals serves to protect and promote the importance of preserving history for future generations. Ongoing tours are available, and all information can be found on their website. The museum today highlights several exhibits dedicated to the spy ring and the Townsend family's contributions to American independence. So, whether you are a history buff, a family looking for an educational experience, or a paranormal enthusiast looking to hopefully capture an apparition or two, Raynham Hall has something to offer everyone.

19
Roxey the LIRR Dog, Mineola, New York

The heartwarming tale of Roxey, an endearing little puppy, originates from the year 1901 when he was discovered journeying solo on the Long Island Railroad. Although there are several different versions of the story of how he got there, it is said that at one of the stops, Garden City, Station Agent Heaney spotted him and brought him into the station. The agent named the puppy Roxey, who eventually became the official mascot of the Long Island Railroad. The adorable terrier-pit bull mix spent the next fourteen years riding on the Long Island Railroad, befriending everyone he met along the way.

Roxey quickly became immensely popular among all the passengers who traveled on the Long Island Railroad. The staff of the railroad took Roxey under their wing, caring for him and ensuring that he was fed. As a result, Roxey, the railroad's official mascot, became the most recognizable and friendly face to everyone he encountered

The president of the Long Island Railroad, Ralph Peters, issued Roxey a special unlimited travel pass that was prominently displayed on his new collar. This pass allowed him to ride all the different branches of the Long Island Railroad. A special name tag was also made and placed on his collar, which read, "I'm Roxey, the LIRR dog. Whose dog are you?"

One of Roxey's favorite stops was Penn Station and each time he arrived, he would be greeted and fed by all his friends at the railroad. Roxey rode the trains across Long Island whenever he pleased. He never missed a connection, never got lost, and always arrived at his intended destination.

Everyone who rode the railroad knew Roxey. One day, President Teddy Roosevelt was riding in his private car on his way to his home in Sagamore Hill. Suddenly, Roxey, entered the car and tried to hop on the president's bed. The crew attempted to remove the dog from the private car, but President Roosevelt instructed them to leave the dog alone and let him stay. He enjoyed being with Roxey and they traveled together all the way to his stop in Oyster Bay.

In 2010, Long Island author Heather Worthington and illustrator Bill Farnsworth immortalized Roxey in their book *Miles of Smiles: The Story of Roxey, the Long Island Railroad Dog*. They celebrated at one of Roxey's favorite spots, Penn Station, with a book signing and a special ceremony.

Roxey the LIRR Dog, Mineola, New York

Roxey. (*Public domain*)

In 1914, Roxey, the dog who was loved so much by so many, passed away at the age of fourteen after falling gravely ill. He was receiving care at an animal hospital in Jamaica, Queens, but unfortunately, he did not recover. One of Roxey's closest friends was a woman named Elsie Hess. She reached out to the LIRR president, Ralph Peters (who was also very fond of Roxey), to ask if Roxey could be buried near the railroad at the Merrick station. Mr. Peters agreed, and the employees of the railroad, along with Ms. Hess, purchased a gravestone that now sits atop Roxey's grave. To this day, people visit Roxey's grave at the Merrick train station building, located on the northeast corner of Merrick Avenue and Sunrise Highway, and often leave flowers to honor his memory.

Roxey's obituary. (*Photo credit: The Brooklyn Daily Eagle 6/12/1914*)

Roxey's grave located at the northside of Sunrise Highway, in the Merrick LIRR station parking lot.

    Donald Lipski is a renowned artist who was approached by the Metropolitan Transit Authority (MTA) to create a unique sculpture at the Mineola station. The station was selected because it had recently undergone the "Third Track Project," which involved demolishing three historical structures to make way for the third track. Lipski loved the story of Roxey from Worthington's book and wanted to do a sculpture of the dog. He began studying deep into the history of Mineola and discovered the town used to have an airfield. He learned that a woman by the name of Bessica "Bessie" Raiche, was the very first woman to fly solo from that airfield on September 16, 1910. She built the plane along with her husband using bamboo and silk.

    At the Mineola station, there is a plaque in her honor addressing her as "The First Woman Aviator of America." She and her husband opened their own company in Mineola which built planes and gave flying lessons. This exceptional woman ended her career in aviation to carry out her other career which was that of an obstetrician/gynecologist in California. Sadly, in 1932, Bessie died from complications of heart disease.

    Deeply moved by both stories, Lipski decided to create a sculpture combining Bessie with Roxey. He used the images from Worthington's book to create Roxey, and his wife, a talented artist and fashion/costume designer, created the artwork for Bessie. Wanting to make sure this was done perfectly, he reached out to master sculptor Christopher Collins from Pennsylvania, who created full-scale plaster models in this Collins Glenside, Pa., studio.

Bessie and Roxey.

Roxey the LIRR Dog, Mineola, New York

Right: Bessie and Roxey.

Below: Bessie holding Roxey's dog tags.

Once the 2,400-pound statue was completed, it was carefully delivered to the Mineola station by way of a flatbed tractor-trailer in preparation for the dedication ceremony, which was scheduled for March 1, 2023.

Lipski's statue pays an amazing and heartwarming tribute to two of the most iconic stories in local aviation history and the history of the Long Island Railroad. Additionally, there is a dedication plaque on the wall of the Mineola station that honors both Bessie Raiche and Roxey, the LIRR dog.

After learning about Roxey's story, I tried to find out if anyone had seen an image of Roxey on any of the trains after his passing, but unfortunately, I could not find any reports. However, if you ever find yourself alone on the LIRR and hear the sound of a dog barking or a dog collar jiggling next to you, it might just be Roxey coming to say hello!

The plaque dedicated to Bessie and Roxey at the Mineola LIRR station.

20

SAGTIKOS MANOR, BAY SHORE, NEW YORK

For decades, tales of hauntings and paranormal phenomena have surrounded Sagtikos Manor, casting a pall of unease over its hallowed halls. Many visitors and residents alike have reported strange occurrences and unexplained sightings within the manor's confines, lending credence to the belief that Sagtikos Manor may be home to restless spirits from ages past.

Sagtikos Manor's origin dates back to the early colonial period of America. The land on which the manor sits was originally inhabited by Native American tribes, primarily the Secatogue tribe, whose name, Sagtikos, means "where the water and land meet." In the seventeenth century, Dutch settlers arrived in the area, establishing farms and homesteads.

The very first resident of Sagtikos Manor was Stephanus Van Cortlandt, the first American-born Mayor of New York City. In 1697, he purchased 145 acres of land from the Secatogue tribe. At that time, the home was built with four rooms and a loft.

In 1758, Abraham Thompson purchased the property which came to approximately 760 acres and had his son, Isaac, manage the land. Isaac married Mary Gardiner, and in 1772, they added ten additional rooms. The Thompson family became integral members of the local community, hosting lavish gatherings and social events at the manor.

The British used it as their headquarters and stayed at the manor for a short time during the American Revolution. It is said that George Washington had spent the night there on April 21, 1790, occupying one of the bedrooms upstairs.

In the late 1800s, Frederick Diodotti Thompson acquired the property and made further renovations. He added forty-two rooms to the manor, which was now on 10 acres of land. The home now included a carriage house, a buttery, a garden, and a family cemetery.

Another prominent inhabitant of Sagtikos Manor and the last of the family to own it was Robert David Lion Gardiner, a descendant of Lion Gardiner, the original English settler of Gardiners Island. Gardiner purchased the manor in 1902 and undertook extensive restoration efforts to preserve its historic integrity. He was deeply enthusiastic about Long Island's history and worked tirelessly to promote its preservation and conservation. He owned the property from 1935 to 1985 when he deeded the property to the Robert David Lion Gardiner Foundation.

There are quite a few haunted legends surrounding Sagtikos Manor that have been handed down over the years. One of the most enduring legends revolves around the

Sagtikos Manor. (*Photo credit: commons.wikimedia.org/wiki/User:DanTD*)

ghost of Winifred Floyd, the daughter of Richard Floyd IV, who is said to roam the halls in search of her lost love. According to local lore, Winifred was forbidden from marrying her true love, a lowly farmhand, and instead was forced to marry a wealthy suitor against her will. Heartbroken and despondent, Winifred is said to have taken her own life within the confines of the manor.

Another legend is the story about the Indian maiden who braved a tremendous storm to save men who were trapped on Fire Island without a way of getting back. In an attempt to get them back safely, she set out on a canoe with two other Indian braves, making several trips back and forth to save all the men. It is said that she never returned from her last trip. People claim to have seen the Indian maiden on the property. Some have claimed to see two men with a canoe. Others have claimed to be able to see the Indian maiden and some of the men she saved standing along the shore.

Another story tells the tale of a woman who was in love and ready to elope with a man who lived nearby. While waiting for her love to pick her up, she was run down and killed. People have claimed to see a woman dressed in white standing alongside the road.

In addition to reported apparitions, visitors claim to have heard disembodied voices in empty rooms, turning doorknobs, and the sound of footsteps. Some believe the spirit of Gardiner is still there. Whether one believes in the existence of ghosts or dismisses such claims as mere superstition, there is no denying the enduring mysteries that lie within the walls of Sagtikos Manor.

Further information about Sagtikos Manor and all tour information can be found on their website. Special events are also posted throughout the year.

The Country House Restaurant, Stony Brook, New York

Located on North Country Road in Stony Brook, stands the quaint Country House Restaurant. Built *circa* 1710, the Country House has seen a lot over the years before becoming a restaurant. It has been a private farmhouse, a town meeting place, a stagecoach stop, as well as a meeting place for George Washington's spies who were part of the Culper Spy Ring during the Revolutionary War. Young Annette Williamson who was murdered in the small dining room of the restaurant called The Old Field Room, is said to haunt the restaurant and is said to be seen all the time, especially by children.

The home was originally built for Obediah Davis who was born about the year 1710. He is said to be originally from Mt. Sinai and then relocated to a two-and-a-half-story home in Stony Brook. The house was tentatively dated back to approximately 1710, but there is some discrepancy as it does not match up to the birth date of Obediah Smith, who was said to have been born around 1710, so it is possible that he acquired the home years later. In 1750, he added the two-story section. He is said to have had two wives and six children: John Davis, Elisabeth Davis, Jonas Davis, Calep Davis, Ruth Davis, and Anne Davis. The home served four generations of the Davis family.

While it was still a farmhouse, it later became occupied by the Williamson family. As the story has it, seventeen-year-old Annette was left to care for the home while her parents had left to secure another property. Since the British troops were advancing, they eventually came to her home and told Annette that they wanted to occupy the house. Annette agreed. The stories say that Annette was put to death by the British for being wrongly accused as a traitor and was hanged upstairs. Her body is said to be buried in the back of the property. As for her parents, they never returned, and it was said they had also been killed.

The house was sold in the 1800s to a famous English actor by the name of Thomas Haddaway. It is said that Haddaway, along with his neighbor, William Sydney Mount, would conduct frequent séances there in an attempt to try to conjure the spirits of the

The Country House Restaurant. (*Photo credit: TheCountryHouseRestaurant.com*)

past.

Over eight years, the restaurant changed names three times. It was the "1710 House" in 1970, and then in 1973, it became "The Hadaway House." Lastly, in 1978, it became "The Country House Restaurant," located on Route 25A and Main Street in Stony Brook, New York.

It is mentioned in the book *Long Island Oddities* that there is a room upstairs that has a narrow door and a small window. This room is rumored to be the old slaves' quarters. A member of the wait staff apparently tried to enter the room, and when he touched the doorknob, he received a horrible shock that radiated up his entire arm to the shoulder, turning it a fiery red. Electricians were called in but could not find anything wrong and had no explanation as to why or how that happened. It is reported that that door has never been opened since that incident and has remained sealed.

There have been claims of footsteps being heard, flashing lights, and the voice of a woman singing has also been heard inside the restaurant. Many believe these strange occurrences are all caused by the ghostly presence of the young blonde-haired girl whose life was taken upstairs, Annette Williamson. Annette has been reportedly seen wearing a white dress, looking out the window on the second floor. Since Annette never knew what had happened to her parents, it is said that she waits by the window for them to return.

The Country House Restaurant is a great location for history, ghostly sightings, strange occurrences, and great food and atmosphere. Here, one can dine in the very rooms where Revolutionary spies might have once exchanged secretive missives, or where Annette Williamson lived her final, fateful days.

22

The Gateway Playhouse, Bellport, New York

The Gateway Playhouse in Bellport is a fascinating place with a rich history that dates back to the early 1800s. Initially constructed as a family farmhouse for Mr. Charles Osborn in 1827, the building underwent several renovations over the years, including an extra wing and ballroom designed by renowned architect Stanford White in 1884. The property changed hands several times until 1941 when Harry Pomeran and his wife, Libby, acquired it with the idea of transforming it into a hotel resort for Christian Scientists visiting Long Island during the summer.

The Pomeran's children, Sally, David, and Ruth, played an instrumental role in running the hotel, serving guests, tending to the family cow, Daisy, drawing water from the well, and ensuring the smooth running and upkeep of the property. They also entertained guests with charming little shows in the dining room, which quickly became popular with the townsfolk. Witnessing the growing admiration for their shows, Harry Pomeran envisioned transforming the barn into a grand theater to showcase even more elaborate performances, thus giving birth to the Gateway Playhouse.

Harry took on the role of producer and dedicated himself to overseeing all the shows, a responsibility he carried out with passion until 1973. Over the years, the playhouse has hosted numerous productions, including plays, musicals, concerts, and comedy shows. The playhouse has also hosted a variety of famous actors, performers, and musicians, including Joan Rivers, Debbie Reynolds, and Tony Bennett, among others.

Despite its rich history and legacy, the Gateway Playhouse has long been rumored to be haunted, with speculation pointing to a possible murder that occurred on the premises back in the late 1800s. Throughout the years, various staff members have reported eerie moans echoing through the halls, leading them to suspect that it might be the ghost of the unfortunate murder victim replaying their final moments. Additionally, sightings of a mysterious figure donning a top hat lurking in the sound booth have been recounted. Strange knocking and tapping noises, along with flickering lights, have also been reported, fueling the spooky atmosphere. Some even suggest that the lingering presence could be none other

The Gateway Playhouse in Bellport, NY. (*Photo credit: DanTDcommons.wikimedia.org/wiki/User:DanTD*)

than the spirit of Lucretia Mott herself, adding to the mystique surrounding the playhouse.

In addition to the usual "resident" spirits that wander around the theater, the Gateway Playhouse also creates one of the top haunted house attractions on Long Island every Halloween. Their team of experts meticulously plans and constructs every section of the haunted house to deliver the most spectacular haunted house experience for all those who visit. Supported by a large and highly skilled group of actors, designers, and staff, they dedicate countless hours to meticulously preparing and practicing to ensure that visitors have a truly unforgettable experience.

Overall, the Gateway Playhouse is a special place that has played a significant role in Bellport's history. Its rich history, legacy, and rumored hauntings make it a fascinating place to visit for anyone interested in theater, history, or the paranormal.

23

THE WICKHAM FARMHOUSE, CUTCHOGUE, NEW YORK

On June 2, 1854, this eighteenth-century, pre-revolutionary home was the site of a brutally vicious axe murder. James and Frances Wickham, owners of the home, were brutally attacked by their former farmhand, twenty-one-year-old Nicholas Behan. Along with the Wickhams, their fourteen-year-old servant boy was also killed.

Nicholas Behan had worked on the Wickham farm for about two years. During his time working on the farm, he met one of the servant girls named Ellen Holland whom he wanted to marry. She rejected his proposal, which enraged Behan, who in turn threatened the young girl for turning down his proposal. Ellen later found out that Behan had gone into her room and stole $10 from her. She reported this to James Wickham who later fired Behan on June 1, 1854. Enraged by the rejection of his proposal and then being fired by the Wickhams, Behan was out for revenge. He returned to the Wickham home around midnight that evening with the intention of raping Ellen Holland first and then killing the Wickhams. When he entered the home, he saw the servant boy, Stephen Winston, asleep and attacked him first. He then went upstairs to the bedroom where James and Frances Wickham were asleep. A violent struggle ensued which was heard by Ellen Holland and another servant girl who were in a nearby room. When they heard the commotion, they escaped out the window to get help. In the meantime, the axe-wielding Behan viciously attacked James and Frances Wickham in one of the most gruesome attacks the town had ever seen.

Desperate at this point, Bain went into a swamp to hide. According to his confession, Bain's plan after the murders was to take the ferry that day from Long Island to New London, CT, and then catch a train to New York City. However, a crowd near the dock made him fear capture. His next plan was to take a train on Long Island to New York, but he was unable to hop onto a box car. That evening, he went to the house of a fellow Irishman in the area to get food, but the man attempted to detain Bain. However, Bain escaped and ran back into the woods. Nicholas Behan had tried to flee on foot while attempting to hide in the wooded swamp areas but was captured by the authorities. He was quickly identified as the murderer as he left his hat at the scene along with a series of very large, bloodied footprints.

The back of the Wickham Farmhouse in Cutchogue. The bedroom where the murders took place in 1854 is at upper left. (*Photo credit: Steve Wick /The Suffolk Times 6/21/18*)

In the years that followed, tales of restless spirits and spectral apparitions would haunt the halls, a grim reminder of the murder that took place in the home. In 1988, Anne and John Wickham, descendants of the ill-fated couple, awoke to a dark figure standing over their bed 124 years after the murder. Petrified, they sealed the room and have not entered since. Some say that you can still hear the footsteps of Nicholas Behan coming from the second-floor hall.

24

VAIL-LEAVITT MUSIC HALL, RIVERHEAD, NEW YORK

Located on Peconic Avenue (originally Bridge Street), the Vail-Leavitt Music Hall in Riverhead was built by David F. Vail and his son, George M. Vail, and was officially opened on October 11, 1881. Since that time, this historic venue has echoed the sounds of countless performances, ranging from high-caliber theatrical productions and vaudeville acts to intimate musical concerts. Originally built by a group of philanthropists, including Franklin O. Vail and P. T. Barnum, the hall was conceived as a community gathering space that would enrich the cultural life of Riverhead. The theatre has also served as a movie theatre. In 1985, it was placed on the National Register of Historic Places.

Originally lit by candlelight, the Vail-Leavitt Music Hall benefited from a gas plant behind the building, which enabled the candles to be replaced with gas fixtures. In 1888, they were able to upgrade to having electricity installed. One can still see some of the original gas jets that were used near the stage below the balcony.

In 1908, George M. Vail, who was now the sole owner of the venue, sold the building to Simon Leavitt. Leavitt was a clothier and tailor, and he leased the upstairs part of the theatre. Simon eventually retired, and his son, Theodore, took over the business. Leavitt's Men's Shop was now located on the ground level of the building, where it became very popular in the community. It was around this time that the Vail-Leavitt Music Hall changed its name to the Lyceum Theater, but years later, it was returned once again to Vail-Leavitt Music Hall.

Hidden behind its doors lies a very long, distinguished, and interesting history. In 1914, Thomas Edison used to conduct his early experiments with sound and film using the Kinetophone inside the theatre, which was the only location where one could visit his exhibits. Unfortunately, in December of that same year, there was a fire in Edison's New Jersey lab, and most of the items pertaining to the Kinetophone were destroyed beyond repair.

The theatre closed at the time of World War I and the flu pandemic. It reopened at the end of World War I, but this time, as a Chinese restaurant called Imperial Restaurant. The music hall suffered a fire from the Chinese kitchen that was on the stage of the theatre and damaged that section of the building. The restaurant closed after that and

Vail-Leavitt Music Hall. (*Photo credit: Americasroof, CC BY-SA 3.0 creativecommons.org/licenses/by-sa/3.0>, via Wikimedia Commons*)

the theatre then changed hands a few times, becoming a pool hall, a betting parlor, a roller-skating rink, and eventually a storage facility for which it remained from the years 1925 to 1978.

The theatre has been undergoing a long restoration process for decades. During the 1980s and up till around 1998, it was once again restored to be used as a theatre and would run showings of old movie classics to help raise funds. In the 2000s, the music hall underwent a major renovation which resulted in a complete overhaul of the music hall. This included the pouring of a new foundation, new carpeting, as well as new heating and air conditioning units. New ceilings were even added which were taken from the original molds. During the overhaul, the original décor was completely maintained.

As a historic location with a vibrant past of over 130 years, one wonders if it could carry over any energy from its past. Over the years, some volunteers have claimed to see dark shadows and hear screams inside the theatre but never found a source that could have caused those to happen.

25

Winfield Hall, Glen Cove, New York

This mansion stands out from the other grand mansions along the Gold Coast due to its truly unique characteristics. Within its walls lie a plethora of enigmatic secrets that belong solely to Frank Winfield Woolworth, secrets that remained hidden and were taken with him to his eternal resting place.

Many of us remember the old "five and dime" stores that were popular back in the day. Also known as "Woolworths," these stores were all owned by business tycoon, Frank Winfield Woolworth and helped generate a $65-million fortune. He spent $13 million to erect the Woolworth Building in Manhattan not to mention his private townhouse on Fifth Avenue. Many of the wealthy business tycoons of that early era of the '20s spent a great deal of their downtime holding lavish parties and living in mansions made of gold and marble. Woolworth was no different and gave just about everything to have the perfect home built in Glen Cove, Long Island. He and his family seemed to have it all—more money than one can dream of—but at what price?

In 1914, Woolworth acquired the 16.5-acre Humphreys Estate on Long Island. After residing there for just two years, a devastating fire ravaged the entire estate. Interestingly, Woolworth already had detailed plans prepared for a new mansion to be built on the property. Around the same time, his townhouse in Manhattan was also under construction and was later sold in 2011 for a staggering $90 million.

Following the tragic fire that consumed his previous home, the construction of Winfield Hall commenced promptly. Woolworth spared no expense in building the grand fifty-seven-room mansion, primarily using marble and limestone. The entire project cost him a modest $9 million upon its completion in 1917. Workers toiled tirelessly day and night, managing to finish the colossal mansion within a mere six months.

Frank W. Woolworth's home life was not only eccentric but incredibly secretive and mysterious as mentioned in numerous books and articles including *Winfield: Living in the Shadow of the Woolworths* by Monica Randall and another detailed history can be found in an article posted on HouseHistree by Mark Meredith on October 10, 2018, and last updated on June 7, 2022. Woolworth and his wife, Jennie Creighton, had three children, all daughters. Jennie had dementia and was losing her grip on reality with each passing day. One of their daughters, Edna, died one night at the Plaza Hotel with her

Right: F. W. Woolworth. (*Public domain*)

Below: One of Woolworth's stores. (*Public domain*)

cause of death listed as "heart failure superinduced by a chronic ear infection." The maid found her on the floor the next morning in pain, but she died immediately after being found and before help could arrive. One of the stories said that Woolworth was hosting a party during a raging thunderstorm. A huge bolt of lightning had struck the marble fireplace, causing a crack right through the family coat of arms that sat upon the mantle. Their coat of arms had the family's likeness on it, and when the lightning bolt struck, it went right through Edna, seemingly leaving the others untouched.

Woolworth was known for being very eccentric. As he got older, his interests in time travel and the occult grew. He also had an obsession with Napolean Bonaparte and felt that he truly was Napolean, reincarnated. The mansion was decorated in mystical motifs containing many Egyptian occult symbols and images of his face with wings on the ceilings. Each one of the bedrooms represented different historical periods such as Ming Dynasty, Elizabethan, Edwardian, Marie Antoinette, etc. Woolworth had a mistress who stayed in the Empress Josephine room which had a secret passageway to his bed chamber. His wife also had her own bedroom, but it was very minimal in comparison to all the others, having one rocking chair and one single bed. Woolworth's own bedroom suite was an identical copy of Napoleon's at Château de Malmaison and the bed was said to actually have belonged to Napolean himself, complete with a canopy made of 14k gold leaf. Crying was often reportedly heard coming from the Marie Antoinette room which has always remained locked and rumored to hold the ghost of his daughter, Edna.

Woolworth designed his own coat of arms, which was carved into the stone above the fireplace. It is probably one of the most bizarre coats of arms ever made. The coat of arms shows Woolworth wearing a plumed helmet with an image of his wife underneath it, an iron mask, and a string of pearls. The faces of all three daughters are on the shield.

The mansion is said to be riddled with trapdoors, secret passages, and hidden tunnels. It also had a private beach, a marble tea house, a golf course, two greenhouses, and an eighteen-car garage. The formal extravagant gardens hold many statues throughout along with a statue of Neptune surrounded by horses carved out of pink marble.

Woolworth did not have much time to enjoy his newly built home; he died a year after Edna's suicide on April 8, 1919, in Winfield Hall, of sepsis from an untreated dental infection. Woolworth had an elaborate mausoleum constructed in Woodlawn Cemetery in the Bronx. It was created to replicate a pharaoh's tomb and bought a sarcophagus where he could lay eternally when the time came. He unfortunately died before the mausoleum was completed but no one knows where he was temporarily laid to rest till it was completed.

Right before Woolworth died, he wrote a will stating that his estate would be distributed to his wife, daughters, grandchildren, friends, and charities, but for whatever reason, he never signed the will. When his wife, Jennie, died, the money was split among their two surviving daughters and to their grandchild, Barbara Hutton Rich, who was the only child born to their deceased daughter Edna. Barbara's inheritance went into a trust, and that was managed by her father, who was a stockbroker and brother to E. F. Hutton. Due to proper management, her $25 million inheritance grew to some $40 million by the time she was twenty-one and received her fortune. Unfortunately, her poor choices in husbands and in money management left her with only $3,000 to her name.

Winfield Hall, Glen Cove, New York

Above left: Jennie Creighton. (*Public domain*)

Above right: Woolworth's daughters, from left to right: Edna, Helena, and Jessie. (*Public domain*)

Right: Obituary of Mrs. Edna Hutton. (*Photo credit: The Sun & NY Press 5/03/1917*)

OBITUARIES.

MRS. EDNA W. HUTTON.

Mrs. Edna W. Hutton, wife of Franklyn L. Hutton of E. F. Hutton & Co., brokers, and daughter of F. W. Woolworth, died suddenly in her apartment in the Hotel Plaza early yesterday morning. Heart trouble, superinduced by a chronic ear affection, was given as the cause of death.

Mrs. Hutton's maid found her mistress lying on the floor, apparently in pain. Dr. Polling Lee, the hotel physician, was summoned, but Mrs. Hutton died in a few minutes. The position in which she was found indicated that she had been trying to get to the window from her bed. Coroner Feinberg said he considered an autopsy unnecessary.

Mr. Hutton was at Bayshore, L. I., preparing the summer home for occupancy when informed of his wife's death. He went to the hotel at once. Mrs. Hutton was 33 years old.

The foyer with marble walls, marble floor, marble staircase, and the custom-designed coat of arms over the fireplace. (*Public domain*)

The house fell to auction in 1925 and was sold to Charles McCann for $395,000. Charles McCann was the husband of Helena, who was Woolworth's oldest daughter. The house stayed in the family for a few more years till it was sold to Julia Louise Parham-Reynolds, the wife of the inventor of Reynolds Wrap foil, Richard S. Reynolds, in 1929. The mansion was sold again in 1963 to Grace Downs Model and Air Career School for girls training to be models and flight attendants from 1963 and 1976. Reportedly, the girls started to notice all the secret rooms and passageways once they started to explore the huge mansion. The girls said they would often hear people talking in rooms that were empty. They began conducting their own séances inside the mansion to see if the spirits would talk to them. In *The Witchery Arts*, author Todd Atteberry writes that on the site, "A secretary staying in the Marie Antionette room woke in the middle of the night by a crying woman, who told her that soon she would be joining her. Within a couple of months, the secretary was dead of a heart attack. A student who smuggled her boyfriend into the house also spent the night in the room, saw that same spirit, and was soon dead in a car crash." Unfortunately, the school was forced to close down after several of the girls died tragically by "bizarre circumstances." It was never clearly defined as to what exactly had happened to them.

Winfield Hall, Glen Cove, New York

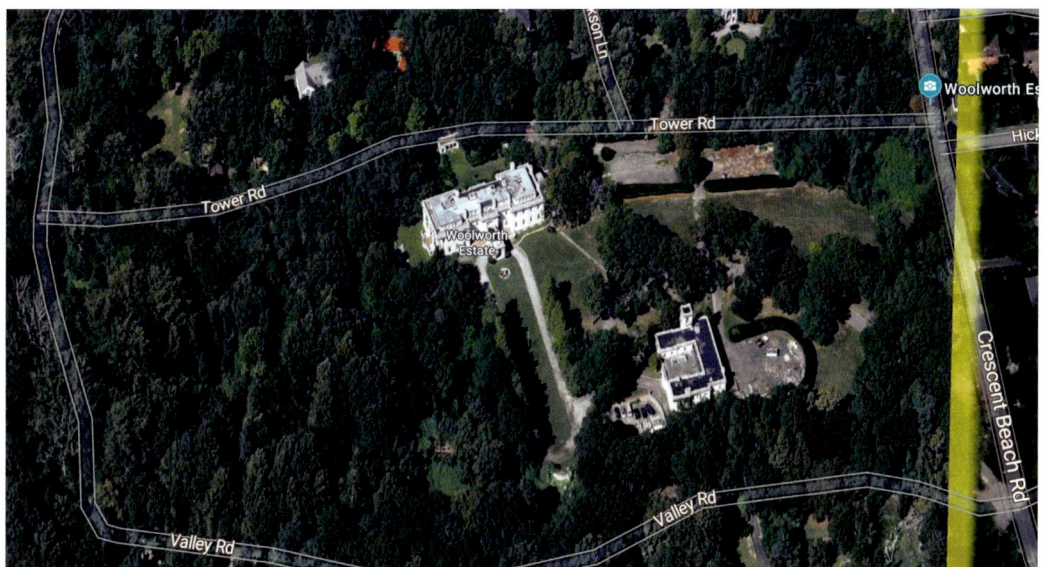

Arial map of Winfield Hall (Woolworth Estate). (*Photo credit: Bing maps*)

The estate once again changed hands and was eventually then owned by Martin Carey and his wife, the same owners of the Seaview Terrace in Rhode Island used in filming *Dark Shadows*. The mansion had changed hands many times and was most recently sold in 2022 to an all-cash buyer from Long Island who remains unknown.

The mansion had always had a strange and unusual feel to it over the years and Woolworth's eccentric tastes and thirst for the occult made it even more hauntingly mysterious. Even Woolworth's daughters had referred to it as a "house of horrors." Rumors of strange noises and talking were heard in empty rooms, and the organ was noted to sometimes play by itself. Some have reported seeing a young girl walking through the gardens. Others have reported hearing the sound of a woman crying on the grounds and also coming from inside the always-locked Antoinette's room. Woolworth had a very strong attraction to the occult and was said to be intrigued by the thought of time travel. Nikola Tesla was on Woolworth's guest list, but it is unknown if he ever provided any funding to Tesla for any of his experiments, especially ones related to time travel. Many wondered what exactly took place in the secret hidden rooms and if any were sealed off.

Winfield Hall is one of the last few remaining Gold Coast mansions from the Gilded Age. It has been used to film *Mildred Pierce* starring Kate Winslet, as well as a video for Taylor Swift, who used the mansion for the inside shots taken in the dining room, fireplace, and main hall for her music video

Since the mansion is privately owned, I doubt a paranormal investigation would be allowed, but if it ever happens, it just might reveal all the secrets it holds behind closed doors.

Bibliography

4girlsandaghost.wordpress.com/2011/10/08/haunted-long-island-winfield-estate/, accessed March 20, 2024

abc7.com/montauk-point-lighthouse-henry-osmers-historian-long-island-history/6430531/, accessed March 22, 2024

allthatsinteresting.com/carl-panzram, accessed March 22, 2024

allthatsinteresting.com/oheka-castle, accessed March 22, 2024

Bayles, R. M., *Historic and Descriptive Sketches of Suffolk County and Its Towns, Villages, Hamlets, Scenery, Institutions, and Important Enterprises* (New York: W. A. Overton, Jr. and Co. 1874)

bestcommunitytheaters.com/place/gateway-playhouse-bellport-ny.html, accessed March 20, 2024

bkps.co/2018/hunting-the-lady-of-the-lake/, accessed March 22, 2024

blogs.shu.edu/litandthecity/2017/12/19/witchcraft-in-new-netherland/, accessed March 22, 2024

books.google.com/books/content?id=ESVEAQAAMAAJ&pg=PA426&img=1&zoom=3&hl=en&sig=ACfU3U24vsZ1mpayTLL4-mQV35HOmEi0pg&ci=25%2C77%2C942%2C364&edge=0, p. 42

brookhavensouthaven.org/helen-tiernan-murder/, accessed March 22, 2024

Burr, G. L., "The New York Cases of Hall and Harrison 1665, 1670" in *Narratives of the Witchcraft Cases 1648–1706* (New York: Charles Scribner's Sons 1914), pp. 39-48

cinematreasures.org/theaters/8610, accessed March 22, 2024

downtownriverhead.org/stop-6, accessed March 22, 2024

Eardeley, W. A., *Rural Cemetery Huntington, Suffolk County Long Island New York* (New York: 1914)

en.wikipedia.org/wiki/Nicholas_Bain, accessed March 20, 2024

executionrocks.wordpress.com, accessed March 22, 2024

facesoflongisland.newsday.com/montauk-lighthouse-keeper-tells-tall-tales-of-history-a-ghost-and-the-next-200-years/, accessed March 22, 2024

Flammer, J., Hill, D., *Long Island's Most Haunted* (PA: Schiffer Publishing 2009)

Gabriel, R. H., *The Evolution of Long Island, A Story of Land and Sea* (London: Humphrey Milford Oxford University Press 1921)

Gethard, C., *Weird New York* (New York: Sterling Publishing Co 2005)

Bibliography

greaterlongisland.com/49602-lakeview-cemetery-stories-about-the-house-on-blood-hill/, accessed March 22, 2024

greaterlongisland.com/cemetery-stories-so-who-were-the-famous-four-sisters-of-patchogue-2/, accessed March 22, 2024

greaterlongisland.com/indian-princess-masterpiece-at-lake-ronkonkoma-awing-visitors/, accessed March 22, 2024

hatchingcatnyc.com/2018/05/20/roxy-long-island-railroad-dog/, accessed March 20, 2024

hauntedhouses.com/new-york/montauk-manor/, accessed March 22, 2024

history.hanover.edu/texts/nyhah.html, accessed March 22, 2024

history.nycourts.gov/case/king-v-hall/, accessed March 22, 2024

historyandheadston.wixsite.com/historyheadstones/post/lakeview-cemetery, accessed March 22, 2024

househistree.com/houses/winfield-hall, accessed March 22, 2024

hoydensandfirebrands.blogspot.com/2012/07/witches-of-new-york.html, accessed March 22, 2024

huntingtonhistory.com/2015/04/, accessed March 22, 2024

huntingtonhistory.com/category/cold-spring-harbor/, accessed March 22, 2024

huntingtonhistory.com/page/6/, accessed March 22, 2024

huntingtonhistory.com/page/6/, accessed March 22, 2024

Jones, W. A, *Long Island* (New York: Baker and Godwin 1863)

Leita, J., Leita, L., *Long Island Oddities* (South Carolina: History Press 2013)

liboatingworld.com/haunted-lighthouses/, accessed March 22, 2024

Long Island Railroad Company, *Out on Long Island* (New York: Charles K. Alley 1890)

longisland.news12.com/long-islands-hidden-past-country-house-restaurant-34740736, accessed March 22, 2024

longisland.news12.com/long-islands-hidden-past-ketcham-inn-in-center-moriches-39220807, accessed March 22, 2024

longislandgenealogy.com/1891/Surnames/H.html, accessed March 22, 2024

longislandgenealogy.com/chapter7.html, accessed March 22, 2024

longislandgenealogy.com/OldHuntington.pdf, accessed March 20, 2024

montaukmanor.com/explore/history/, accessed March 22, 2024

newhorizonsgenealogicalservices.com/rev-ny-suffolk-buried.htm, accessed March 22, 2024

nyheritage.contentdm.oclc.org/digital/search/collection/p15281coll78/searchterm/Ed%20Crasky%20Montauk%20Air%20Force%20Station%20Photographs/field/relatig/mode/exact/conn/and/order/date/ad/asc, accessed March 20, 2024

nyheritage.org/collections?search_api_fulltext=long%20island%20music%20halls&page=6, accessed March 20, 2024

nyheritage.org/collections?search_api_fulltext=long%20island%20music%20halls&page=7, accessed March 20, 2024

nyheritage.org/collections?search_api_fulltext=suffolk+county+court+1854, accessed March 20, 2024

nypost.com/2018/10/30/the-haunted-tale-that-keeps-long-island-locals-out-of-this-lake/, accessed March 22, 2024

nypost.com/article/camp-hero-montauk-project-conspiracy/, accessed March 20, 2024

oakmonitoronline.com/11763/uncategorized/the-strange-sites-of-long-island/, accessed March 20, 2024

Panchyk, R., *Hidden History of Long Island* (South Carolina: History Press 2016)

Parishes, Mid-Winter Fete, "Nathan Hale, Battle of Long Island" in *Long Island Calendar 1902*, (New York: The Orphans Press 1902), pp. 123,147-151

parlorofhorror.wordpress.com/2013/08/29/the-old-burying-ground-and-tombstone-bread/, accessed March 22, 2024

parlorofhorror.wordpress.com/2013/08/29/the-old-burying-ground-and-tombstone-bread/, accessed March 22, 2024

parlorofhorror.wordpress.com/tag/fort-golgotha/, accessed March 22, 2024

patch.com/new-york/huntington/a-new-view-civil-war-memories, accessed March 22, 2024

patch.com/new-york/huntington/a-new-view-mount-misery, accessed March 22, 2024

patch.com/new-york/huntington/bp--ghosts-from-the-whaling-days, accessed March 22, 2024

patch.com/new-york/huntington/bp--long-islands-legends-and-myths-part-iii-sweet-hollow-road, accessed March 22, 2024

patch.com/new-york/huntington/bp--the-wickham-murders-of-1854, accessed March 20, 2024

patch.com/new-york/huntington/bp--the-wickham-murders-of-1854, accessed March 20, 2024

patch.com/new-york/huntington/bp--the-wickham-murders-of-1854, accessed March 22, 2024

patch.com/new-york/huntington/fort-golgotha-at-the-old-burial-grounds, accessed March 22, 2024

patch.com/new-york/riverhead/ghostly-activity-peaks-at-vail-leavitt-music-hall, accessed March 22, 2024

patch.com/new-york/sachem/the-legends-of-lake-ronkonkoma, accessed March 22, 2024

patch.com/new-york/sayville/long-islands-own-witchcraft-trial-1657, accessed March 22, 2024

pbase.com/jimrob/winfieldhall, accessed March 20, 2024

Pelletreau, W. S., *Records of the Town of Smithtown, Long Island, N.Y. with Other Ancient Documents of Historic Value* (New York: Long Islander Print 1898)

Platt, H. C., *Old Times in Huntington, an Historical Address* (New York: Long Islander Print 1876)

Prime, N. S., "Section IX Trials for Witchcraft" in *A History of Long Island From Its First Settlement by Europeans to the Year 1815* (New York: Robert Carter 1845), pp. 88-90

projects.newsday.com/lifestyle/haunted-long-island-fire-island-lighthouse/, accessed March 22, 2024

Radall, M., *Winfield: Living in the Shadow of the Woolworths* (New York: Thomas Dunne Books 2003)

Rattray, J. E., *East Hampton History Including Geneologies of Early Families* (New York: Country Life Press 1953)

rephotogenica.wordpress.com/2011/06/14/historycrawl/, accessed March 22, 2024

Sforza, Dr. A., Mattheou, A. S., *Images of America Around Huntington Village* (South Carolina: Arcadia Publishing 2013)

sisfg.com/the-woolworth-misfortune-how-not-to-provide-for-heirs , accessed March 22, 2024

sites.google.com/site/longislandstories/patchogue-stories, accessed March 22, 2024

sites.google.com/site/longislandstories/the-harts-tavern-mystery, accessed March 22, 2024

sites.google.com/site/longislandstories/the-traveling-dead-of-patchogue, accessed March 22, 2024

sites.google.com/site/longislandstories/whos-haunting-lakeview-cemetery, accessed March 22, 2024

smithtownhistorical.org/historical-buildings/, accessed March 20, 2024

suburbanfiremarshal.org/?p=9817, accessed March 22, 2024

suffolktimes.timesreview.com/2018/06/north-fork-history-project-murders-1854-shattered-hamlet/, accessed March 20, 2024

Bibliography

suffolktimes.timesreview.com/2018/06/north-fork-history-project-murders-1854-shattered-hamlet/, accessed March 22, 2024

suffolktimes.timesreview.com/2018/07/north-fork-history-project-wickham-murders-part-two-field-hand-exacts-revenge/, accessed March 20, 2024

suffolktimes.timesreview.com/2018/07/north-fork-history-project-wickham-murders-part-two-field-hand-exacts-revenge/, accessed March 22, 2024

tbrnewsmedia.com/guided-tour-of-huntingtons-old-burying-ground-offers-insight-into-towns-historic-past/, accessed March 22, 2024

The Long Island Railroad Company, *Long Island* (New York: The Aldin Press 1882), pp. 13-16, 36

Thompson, B. F., "Suffolk County" in *History of Long Island Containing An Account of the Discovery and Settlement With Other Important Matters* (New York: E. French 1938), pp. 152-167

timesmachine.nytimes.com/timesmachine/1854/06/06/75433627.pdf, accessed March 20, 2024

timesmachine.nytimes.com/timesmachine/1854/06/07/97114360.pdf, accessed March 20, 2024

torontodreamsproject.blogspot.com/2020/02/north-americas-first-valentine-when.html, accessed March 22, 2024

Townsend, M., Townsend-Townshend 1066–1909, *The History, Genealogy and Alliances of The English and American House of Townsend* (New York: LC 1909)

troytaylorbooks.blogspot.com/2013/02/popper-poltergeist.html

untappedcities.com/2018/05/25/a-memorial-to-roxey-the-canine-mascot-of-the-long-island-railroad/, accessed March 20, 2024

untappedcities.com/2021/11/29/places-to-discover-in-huntington/4/, accessed March 22, 2024

usghostadventures.com/haunted-stories/execution-rocks-a-dark-lighthouse/, accessed March 22, 2024

vail-leavittmusichall.godaddysites.com/vail-leavitt-history, accessed March 22, 2024

washingtonspytrail.com/the-country-house/, accessed March 22, 2024

weirdus.com/states/new_york/road_less_traveled/mount_misery_road/index.php, accessed March 22, 2024

westbullseye.com/2101/in-depth/history-of-long-island-from-montauk-to-manhattan-myths-and-haunted-places/, accessed March 22, 2024

wheresthedrama.wordpress.com/2013/01/07/haunted-eateries-of-long-island/, accessed March 22, 2024

wildabouthere.com/137-steps-montauk-point-lighthouse/, accessed March 22, 2024

www.27east.com/home-garden/true-crime-on-the-north-fork-the-wickham-axe-murders-1390346/, accessed March 22, 2024

www.americanhauntingsink.com/popper, accessed March 20, 2024

www.architecturaldigest.com/story/everything-you-need-to-know-about-long-islands-oheka-castle, accessed March 22, 2024

www.broadwayworld.com/long-island/article/Bellports-Gateway-Playhouse-Keeps-Rolling-Along-20080707, accessed March 20, 2024

www.cutchoguenewsuffolkhistory.org/news/were-there-witches-on-the-east-end/, accessed March 22, 2024

www.cutchoguenewsuffolkhistory.org/timeline/the-wickham-farmhouse-1704/, accessed March 20, 2024 www.cutchoguenewsuffolkhistory.org/timeline/the-wickham-farmhouse-1704/, accessed March 22, 2024

www.danspapers.com/2011/10/spookiness-in-montauk-why-did-the-radar-dish-at-camp-hero-just-turn-to-face-south/, accessed March 20, 2024

www.danspapers.com/2018/10/haunted-hamptons-2/, accessed March 22, 2024

www.danspapers.com/2020/02/historic-axe-murders-re-examined/, accessed March 20, 2024

www.danspapers.com/2020/02/historic-axe-murders-re-examined/, accessed March 22, 2024

www.danspapers.com/2021/12/the-montauk-lighthouse-history/, accessed March 22, 2024

www.danspapers.com/2023/12/new-vail-leavitt-music-hall-riverhead/, accessed March 22, 2024

www.dar.org/library/research-guides/long-island-and-nyc-rev-war-resources, accessed March 22, 2024

www.deboradale.com/old-bethpage-hauntings/, accessed March 20, 2024

www.discoverlongisland.com/blog/stories/post/spooky-historic-sites-paranormal-experiences-around-long-island/, accessed March 20, 2024

www.facebook.com/100057364783036/posts/the-montauk-lighthouse-is-haunted-by-a-17-year-old-girl-abigail-the-most-famous-/357554479500…, accessed March 22, 2024

www.fancypantshomes.com/luxury/winfield-hall-the-historic-woolworth-mansion-in-glen-cove/, accessed March 20, 2024

www.findagrave.com/cemetery/2348590/memorial-search?firstname=&middlename=&lastname=&cemeteryName=Obediah+Davis+Cemetery&…, accessed March 22, 2024

www.findagrave.com/memorial/1127/frank_winfield_woolworth, accessed March 20, 2024

www.findagrave.com/memorial/29922938/ebenezer-prime, accessed March 20, 2024

www.findagrave.com/memorial/40267853/karl-h-klein, accessed March 22, 2024

www.findagrave.com/memorial/52061516/jennie-woolworth, accessed March 20, 2024

www.girlwiththepassport.com/haunted-hotels-in-new-york/, accessed March 22, 2024

www.goldcoastmansions.com/WinfieldHall/WinfieldHall.htm, accessed March 20, 2024

www.gothichorrorstories.com/gothic-travel/by-location/mid-atlantic/long-island/country-house-restaurant-ghost-stony-brook/, accessed March 22, 2024

www.gothichorrorstories.com/gothic-travel/the-ghosts-of-fire-island-lighthouse/, accessed March 22, 2024

www.gothichorrorstories.com/journal/the-legends-and-myths-of-sweet-hollow-and-mount-misery-a-long-island-mystery/, accessed March 22, 2024

www.gothichorrorstories.com/journal/winfield-hall-what-are-the-mysterious-secrets-of-f-w-woolworths-haunted-long-island-home/, accessed March 20, 2024

www.gothichorrorstories.com/journal/winfield-hall-what-are-the-mysterious-secrets-of-f-w-woolworths-haunted-long-island-home/, accessed March 20, 2024

www.gothichorrorstories.com/new-york/the-ghosts-of-old-bethpage-village-restoration/, accessed March 20, 2024

www.historichotels.org/us/hotels-resorts/oheka-castle/?from=rezconsole, accessed March 22, 2024

www.history.navy.mil/research/library/online-reading-room/title-list-alphabetically/p/philadelphia-experiment.html, accessed March 20, 2024

www.hmdb.org/m.asp?m=144981, accessed March 22, 2024

www.hmdb.org/m.asp?m=175639, accessed March 22, 2024

www.hmdb.org/m.asp?m=175642, accessed March 22, 2024

www.hmdb.org/m.asp?m=175679, accessed March 22, 2024

www.hmdb.org/m.asp?m=213358, accessed March 22, 2024

www.hmdb.org/results.asp?Search=Place&Town=Cutchogue&State=New York, accessed March 22, 2024

www.hotelnewsresource.com/article85244.html, accessed March 22, 2024

www.huntingtonhistoricalsociety.org/hhs-blog, accessed March 22, 2024

www.interment.net/data/us/ny/suffolk/old-burying-ground/index.htm, accessed March 22, 2024

www.ipernity.com/doc/laurieannie/24038185, accessed March 20, 2024

www.lighthousefriends.com/light.asp?ID=749, accessed March 20, 2024

www.lihauntedhouses.com/real-haunt/montauk-manor.html, accessed March 22, 2024

www.lihauntedhouses.com/real-haunt/old-bethpage-village-restoration.html, accessed March 20, 2024

www.lihauntedhouses.com/real-haunt/stony-brook-grist-mill.html, accessed March 20, 2024

www.lihauntedhouses.com/real-haunt/sweet-hollow-road.html, accessed March 22, 2024

www.liherald.com/stories/who-really-owned-the-inn-in-east-meadow,126738, accessed March 20, 2024

www.longisland.com/news/07-17-19/5-stories-about-ufo-encounters-on-long-island.html, accessed March 22, 2024

www.longisland.com/news/09-10-23/seven-times-oheka-castle-was-featured-in-a-movie-show-or-music-video.html, accessed March 22, 2024

www.longisland.com/news/10-26-20/five-crazy-scary-facts-legends-stories-about-long-island.html, accessed March 22, 2024

www.longisland.com/news/10-26-20/five-crazy-scary-facts-legends-stories-about-long-island.html, accessed March 22, 2024

www.longisland.com/news/10-26-20/five-crazy-scary-facts-legends-stories-about-long-island.html, accessed March 22, 2024

www.longisland.com/news/10-31-19/a-witch-hunt-on-long-island-colonial-era-controversy-in-east-hampton-predated-salem-trials.html?print=1&…, accessed March 22, 2024

www.longisland.com/news/11-27-19/crazy-facts-about-lake-ronkonkoma.html, accessed March 22, 2024

www.longisland.com/news/12-11-19/crazy-facts-about-the-fire-island-lighthouse.html, accessed March 22, 2024

www.longislandgenealogy.com/lighthouse.html, accessed March 22, 2024

www.longislandhistoryproject.org/floyds-like-us/, accessed March 22, 2024

www.longislandpress.com/2019/10/28/witch-trials-hexing-in-the-hamptons/, accessed March 22, 2024

www.maggieblanck.com/Land/SmithtownTS.html, accessed March 22, 2024

www.mountvernon.org/library/digitalhistory/digital-encyclopedia/article/culper-spy-ring/, accessed March 22, 2024

www.newsday.com/lifestyle/family/montauk-lighthouse-ghosts-abigail-v38818, accessed March 22, 2024

www.newsday.com/lifestyle/holidays/halloween/haunted-long-island-y75638, accessed March 20, 2024

www.newsday.com/lifestyle/holidays/halloween/haunted-long-island-y75638, accessed March 22, 2024

www.newsday.com/long-island/towns/vail-leavitt-music-hall-riverhead-tds58d4d, accessed March 22, 2024 www.newsday.com/news/smithtown-seniors-gather-for-a-walk-down-memory-lane-t17299, accessed March 22, 2024

www.newyorkhauntedhouses.com/real-haunt/lake-ronkonkoma.html, accessed March 22, 2024

www.newyorkhauntedhouses.com/real-haunt/old-burial-hill-cemetery.html, accessed March 22, 2024

www.newyorkhauntedhouses.com/real-haunt/sweet-hollow-road.html, accessed March 22, 2024

www.nps.gov/fiis/learn/historyculture/fire-island-lighthouse-history.htm, accessed March 22, 2024

www.nps.gov/fiis/planyourvisit/fireislandlighthouse.htm, accessed March 22, 2024

www.oheka.com/history.htm, accessed March 22, 2024

www.patchoguecemetery.org/history 1/4, accessed March 22, 2024

www.ronkonkomachamber.com/myths-legends, accessed March 22, 2024

www.smithsonianmag.com/history/before-salem-there-was-the-not-so-wicked-witch-of-the-hamptons-95603019/, accessed March 22, 2024

www.thetravel.com/execution-rocks-lighthouse-dark-history/, accessed March 22, 2024

www.threevillagehistoricalsociety.org/post/witchcraft-in-setauket-the-trial-of-ralph-and-mary-hall, accessed March 22, 2024

www.trains.com/trn/railroads/history/bessie-and-roxey-statue-at-mineola-station/, accessed March 20, 2024

www.tumblr.com/acrossthewavesoftime/676160578509783040/to-you-my-heart-i-must-resign-o-choose-me-for, accessed March 20, 2024

www.vanderbiltcupraces.com/blog/article/mystery_foto_friday_59_can_you_identify_this_hotel_and_autos, accessed March 22, 2024

www.visithistoriclongisland.com/Sagtikos_Manor.html, accessed March 22, 2024

www.weirdus.com/states/new_york/local_legends/lady_of_lake_ronkonkoma/index.php, accessed March 22, 2024

www.wikitree.com/wiki/Davis-52454, accessed March 22, 2024